NATALIE,

THANK YOU FOR YOUR SUPPORT
I HOPE YOU ENJOY THE BOOK

A BETTER LIFE

The Autobiography of
Anthony A. Crutchfield III

PREFACE

I always knew I wanted a better life, but I never realized how much I wanted it until I wrote my autobiography. The decision to write this autobiography was not exactly planned. A friend who knew about my life asked me to tell my story at a TED Talk. This suggestion caught me by surprise because it was pointing me in a direction where it did not seem to follow the path my life was heading at that point. After my heart convinced my brain that I could do it, one thing led to another and I became riveted to the need to document more of my early childhood. The Ted Talk soon became secondary as the energy and enthusiasm for recording the events that unfolded in my life consumed much of my time. I felt compelled to continue on this new path that my life was headed and to see where it would lead. Gradually it became clear to me that I could use my life experiences to help others who were less fortunate.

Some special people must be credited for not only playing a significant role in my life but also for the critical part they knowingly or unknowingly played in shaping the character of the man I've become today. I also discovered from my research the unanswered questions and some unspoken secrets that were revealed long after some life changing events occurred. Events that dictated the direction that my siblings and I would take and which drew all the inner strengths that any young impressionable youth can gather. Much of my source for my story came from my mother. In reading and recollecting the life that I was forced to accept, I cannot at this point of my life hold any bitterness towards my mother, in fact I recognize now that many of the decisions she made that changed her life forever were as a result of a broken home environment which she was also forced to endure; until she could no longer take the abuse. My father Tony entered her life at this most vulnerable stage with an offer that she felt was her best option to take her out of a home that did not have the love or support that she needed so badly. Little did she know that this decision would cause her a life that she felt was going to be better. Throughout the book, my mother remained for the most part of my life the stabilizing force that kept me grounded in many ways; tough at the same time myself and my siblings felt that many of the decisions she made catapulted our young lives to the point where we never knew where we would land. Writing this book has reaffirmed my strong belief that regardless of some bad decisions made throughout my young life that affected me, I always felt that I could have 'a better life'.

For Enga my mother, being strong was in most cases all she had to keep her going. Being consumed by drugs at an early age immediately made her dependent and her life from then on was not her own. Living in this environment made me determined that I was not going to give my life up to anyone or anything, much less drugs, to take control of my thoughts or my life... I just knew there had to be 'a better life'. I now realize that drug addiction is a disease. A disease my mother fought for years, and it appears that she has won her battle. I am glad that she found it within herself to love herself and leave the past behind. Nothing good comes out of drug use.

As a young boy, growing up in an uncertain environment is very challenging. I never knew what lay ahead, but what I do know is, had it not been for the support of some members of my family and friends along the way to help guide my character, I would not be the strong successful person I am today. A person who was able to determine the people that were the positive forces in my life. Like an Aunt who showed me that there were other choices in life besides the one I inherited from the day I was born. The woman who I chose to be my wife, because I instinctively knew after I met her that her mental and ethical traits were the qualities I needed in a partner in my quest for a better life. Because I have had to accept so much in my young life I have developed a high level of tolerance, which allows me to be more accepting of differences and less prejudiced.

This autobiography attempts to offer lessons I have learned in my life that has led o much of my successes. Success or failure in any situation or endeavors depends, more than anything else, on how we respond to circumstances or events. It is our character that determines our success. That is not to say that 'good' people will always experience success than 'bad' people. However there are some character traits that lead to 'successes' and other traits that lead to 'failures'. Truth is if I were to break down 'honesty' which is a 'good' character trait, it would consist of several other qualities like truthfulness and dependability. Therefore, I worked at becoming more honest, which at the same time helped me to become more truthful and more dependable. The events I have shared with you could easily have broken me, but I chose to use them to make me stronger and more determined to find that better life we all want. I am now convinced that in sharing I can play a positive role in helping the youth to understand that character guides your responses to any situation or circumstances in your life.

I have had the assistance of my family, friends, colleagues and professionals who have helped me complete this autobiography and to whom I express my appreciation. The advice and support I received is immeasurable. The encouragement I have received has reaffirmed my belief that in sharing the ups and downs of my life, you will be inspired to not let anything or anyone hold you back and to help our at-risk youth attain A Better Life. Success requires effort, persistence and patience, and eventually it does pay off.

1

Tony and Enga the beginning

It's not often that you get to tell your story to the world and start off from the very beginning, where your parents met to later create you. That's where I am starting with my story. My parents fell in love despite being different in some ways. But it was what they found in common that brought them together. My dad's name is Tony and he was known to be the coolest dude in school. He was 5'9" and 125 pounds of pure handsomeness. Unfortunately, he dropped out of school before he even finished the sixth grade. His restless boyhood led him to feel as if the walls of the school would suffocate him if he did not get out. He was not one to be confined and conformed... even in school.

Back in 1963, when my parents Julia Carter aka Enga and Tony Crutchfield met, Enga was in the eighth grade attending Lewis Junior High School and Tony made a habit of hanging out at the school when it had let out. He had friends there but despite his popularity, he was lonely throughout the day. Life out of school wasn't what he thought it was going to be. It was much tougher but his pride prevented him from attending school again. When Enga entered her freshman year at the Jeremiah E. Burke High School in Boston, Tony seized the moment and approached her rather confidently with his hands thrust deep inside of his worn out jeans pocket.

"Enga, you are so beautiful!" Tony exclaimed.

Upon receiving an encouraging look from an impressionable Enga, he continued "Can we talk soon; I would love to get to know you better". They immediately exchanged numbers but somehow never found time to see each other. One Saturday night they both attended a party not knowing that the other was going to be there. A suave Tony approached Enga who was once again captivated by his confidence. In that moment where the rhythm of the music seemed to pump the adrenalin in her body to a high, which sent inexplicable emotions to her brain; she did all she could to restrain from throwing her body into Tony's as he asked her to dance.

From that night on there was an instant connection which unknown to them would spiral their lives into a roller coaster ride of a lifetime. After a couple of months of dating, Tony felt confident enough to share a proposal with Enga, one that he felt she could not resist.

He had a gift of the gab and could sell ice to an Eskimo plus his confidence didn't hurt either. His plan was for Enga to drop out of school and the two of them would put her body up for sale. This would become known as the "family business". Enga stood 4'11" tall, weighing 125 pounds, had a light caramel complexion, a perfect figure and being from Puerto Rico she had a strong Spanish accent. In those days light skin was "in" and Tony believed that he struck gold with my mother.

Enga was in a desperate state of mind during this time. She was praying for a way to get out of her mother's home, so when Tony came up with this idea, she figured her prayers were answered and this was the only way out. She had made up her mind that she was not going to take any more of the physical abuse that my grandmother Matilda subjected her to. If Matilda came home and the dishes were not done, she would brutally beat Enga with frying pans and pots all the while yelling at her in Spanish "pedazo de mierda" which translates to "you're a piece of shit". There would be times when my grandmother would beat her until she broke skin and saw blood. If Enga came home speaking Spanish, Matilda would punch her in the mouth so hard that her teeth would cut into her lips and blood would pour from her mouth.

An angry Matilda had exclaimed to Enga,

"I will Americanize you. People here in the United States don't speak Spanish, and neither will you, as long as you are in this house!"

It was no wonder that Enga could not stop thinking about Tony's proposal. One day she came home and as she stepped foot in the door she was beaten again; this time it was because the bathroom was not cleaned to Matilda's specifications. It was at this point that Enga decided that Tony's proposal was her only option and dropped out of school to start working in "The Family Business", also known as prostitution. For five years the family business thrived, and in December of 1968 Enga got pregnant. When they received the news that she was pregnant Enga stopped working the streets, and Tony was able to find a job as a cook at a local diner. He worked 40 hours a week to provide for his new family. In September of 1969, she gave birth to my older brother, Aaron. At this point, the doctor told Enga that she had to abstain from sex for six weeks.

With additional mouths to feed, Tony started to count down the days and weeks until Enga could return to work and earn them money like they originally had planned. As soon as Enga went back to work Tony quit his job and began to manage the finances of the business.

4

Seeing the money rolling in, it did not take Tony very long for greed to manifest itself; he wanted more. Being the smooth talker that he was for his young age, Tony was able to convince two other girls, Corrine and Sheri-Ann to join his "stable". Together with Enga, the girls worked daily, they didn't believe in having days off, especially on the weekend. The weekend was when they made most of their money. Tony managed the profits, and also disciplined the girls when he felt it was necessary which meant occasional threats and beatings.

Planned Parenthood was not a factor in those days; therefore it was no surprise that in January 1970, Enga became pregnant again with my sister Natasha. During this pregnancy Tony didn't have to get a job because he had the other girls working for him. My sister Natasha was born in Oct of 1970. In February of 1971, Tony became addicted to heroin and found himself in jail at the Charles Street jail for drug possession. Enga held the family business together in his absence; unfortunately she got pregnant by one of her "John's" and gave birth to her third child named Kim. When Tony got out of jail he ran into Enga on the corner of Massachusetts Avenue and Washington Street in Roxbury pushing her new baby in a cheap stroller while Aaron and Natasha walked beside her. When he saw the newest addition to his family, Tony got enraged and started to punch and kick Enga. Grabbing a wooden stick lying on the ground, he continued beating her totally oblivious to the other kids witnessing this brutal assault. Fearing for her life, she managed to run while the kids stood motionless and in shock. As she ran away, Tony drew a 32-caliber handgun he carried for protection, pointed it at Enga and pulled the trigger. Unfortunately the bullet struck her in the leg but it could have been much worst. When the police came and asked who shot her, she told the police she had no idea who the assailant was. It was not surprising that the shooter was never found by the police. Shortly after, an ambulance arrived and drove her two blocks to Boston City Hospital. She stayed in the hospital for four days while she received treatment for her gunshot wound. When she was released, Enga was faced with no choice but to return to the only home she knew, the home she shared with Tony.

Although Tony was able to quench his sexual thirst with the other girls of the organization, one day in early February he decided to reacquaint himself with Enga. Having been shot by him, and still healing, she resisted. Unfortunately, Tony wasn't in the mood to take "No", for an answer. After being beaten for a while, she stopped fighting and gave in to his sexual demands. These forced sexual encounters were technically rapes and were the resulting moments of my existence, which ten months later led to my birth into this wonderful, loving family.

Although Tony took care of Kim, he never accepted her. When I was about 9 months old, Tony the callous street hustler, met someone that was very interested in buying Kim. This was an opportune time as apparently there were very few white babies available for adoption. When my grandmother Anne Hill, Tony's mother, discovered that Tony was trying to sell Kim she told Enga knowing that she would want to take Kim and run. Anne told Enga that she would save Kim under two conditions. Seeing that Anne never really cared for Enga, it was no surprise that her first condition was that Enga leave Tony and the state. The second condition was less predictable. My grandmother said Enga would have to leave Kim with her to serve as a sort of indentured servant. If Enga did not agree to this, Anne said she would allow Tony to sell Kim and no one would ever see her again. Anne was a diabetic, poor and lonely. She had three children, but in her old age, she grew to be a mean woman and only had visitors out of necessity. Having to decide between never seeing Kim again and indentured servitude was an impossible choice. Initially, Enga figured she would simply take her kids and run from Tony as she did many times before. The problem was that every time Enga ran, Tony was able to find her. Obviously, Tony knew if Enga was aware of his plan to sell Kim, there was nothing she wouldn't do to stop him. Regretfully, Enga agreed to leave Kim with Anne. She then reached out to Corrine, one of the working girls from Boston, who now lived in California. In 1974, having stopped the sale of Kim, while banishing her into indentured servitude, Enga moved to California with the rest of her kids to live with Corrine until she could find a place of her own. Within a few months the rest of us were living in California, minus Kim.

2

Welcome to California

Meanwhile back in Boston Tony had a friend who lived in Atlanta, Georgia who was willing to buy guns in Georgia and bring them to Boston on the Amtrak train. Once in Boston, Tony and another friend would sell the guns and the three of them would split the profit. These were not just regular guns. He would sell fully automatic machine-guns and silencers; and they even got a hold of some military grenades. One day a guy approached Tony and placed a large order. After taking the order, the gun connection in Georgia got arrested and therefore they couldn't fulfill the order. By this time, Tony's heroin addiction grew stronger and as expected the money to support his addiction was diminishing. Since Tony and the friend in Boston knew the buyer would have cash on him to pay for the guns he intended to purchase, they decided to set up a meeting with the buyer and rob him. Tony and his friend already had guns, and presumably the buyer didn't. If things went the way he planned, he would have thousands of dollars on hand, enough money to last several months.

They decided to meet the buyer in a field near Center Street in Roxbury. They got there about two hours early in an attempt to set up their plan, however the buyer was apparently smarter than they were and was already there waiting for them. Tony and his friend walked up to him and after exchanging pleasantries, pulled out their guns and instructed the buyer to give up the money. At that point, The Boston Police, The Massachusetts State Police, FBI and ATF all came at him from every direction on horses and motorcycles, in cars and on foot. Tony would later say that he thought some even rose from the ground. The buyer turned out to be an ATF agent who had been investigating Tony for quite some time. Tony and his partner were arrested and charged with armed robbery of an ATF agent and sentenced to 10 years in prison. Tony ended up doing an additional five years because he escaped from prison.

Tony's "escape" happened in 1975. During his time in prison he became a model inmate earning the respect of all the guards. He was a gifted speaker, very convincing and always respectful, polite and easy going. It was not surprising that people seemed to always want to be in his company. He had gotten really good with getting people to follow him. Usually it was women, now it was the guards that fell into his charismatic trap. One day the warden approached Tony and explained to him that he was developing a work release program where inmates would leave the jail in the morning for work and return to the jail after their shift was complete.

Being a model inmate, a guard recommended Tony for the program. Tony was excited and agreed to join the program. Sometime later, the warden got him a job as a cook in a local diner, at this point, the only real job Tony ever had was as a cook. For months, he would leave the jail in the morning, and go to work, once his shift was over, he would take public transportation back to the jail. When he returned to the jail he was searched thoroughly, to ensure that he had no contraband. He noticed that the longer he was in this program, the less the guards searched him. They started to trust him more and more as time went on. Other inmates saw how freely he came and went into the jail and the inmates started to request that he sneak things into the jail for them. Being the people person that he was, it did not take much convincing to get him to agree. The main request made of him was for drugs. The problem was that he never knew when he would be searched. Therefore, he had to hide the drugs in the only place he knew they were less likely to look, in his rectum.

For months he got away with this, until one day he refused an inmate's request. Coincidentally, the next week, when he returned to the jail, the warden was at the front door waiting for him. The inmate had snitched on him. Tony was handcuffed; they conducted a full body search, and found the cocaine he was bringing in. Even though he did not technically escape, the charge was the same. They also charged him with introducing contraband into a jail and a number of other things. Needless to say, the work release program was cancelled for all inmates.

Meanwhile, back in California, Enga, who was 29 years old, started to date Corrine's 19 year old son Eric. Surprisingly, Corrine was very supportive of their relationship. Corrine was like an aunt to me. I spent many nights at her house. She would have me sit on her lap and steer the wheel of the car as she worked the gas and brake. When I wanted to get away for a night or weekend, it was Corrine that I called. Sometimes she came and got me and we just hung out at her house or even at her job. I felt like I was her favorite. When we got our own apartment, Eric moved in with us and he became the first father figure I knew. Eric and Enga started to sell marijuana and with the money they received, they were able to buy a house in Compton.

At that time, Compton was an upper middle class community with mostly people of color. The house was a three bedroom, single story house with an unattached garage and a good amount of land. Aaron and I shared one room, Natasha had a room to herself and Enga and Eric shared the last room. In the garage, we had a pool table and a small weight room complete with heavy bag and speed bag. Eric had quite a few friends that would come over and hang out. One guy came and worked out daily, he was as big as the Incredible Hulk. They called him "Niggaplease". I could never figure out how someone could earn such a name, but I wasn't brave enough to ask. Even though I was a child of less than eight years old, I got really good at playing pool. I got so good that once it was my turn to shoot, my opponent rarely got another chance. I'd knock all my balls into the pockets. We had a large front yard and a small back yard. Our dining room had mirrors on all of the walls from floor to ceiling. It was large enough for a piano to fit on one wall and a six-person dining room table to fit comfortably in the room. Our front room was much larger, with a 10x10 window within the wall leading out to the porch in the front of the house facing the street. We also had a fresh water fish tank built into the wall separating my room from the hallway. At the end of the long hallway that led to

13

the rear bedrooms, was a two-way radio, which Eric used to talk to truck drivers for fun.

 We had a pit bull named Bear that was like one of the family. Bear was small, but fierce. Eric used to put hot pepper in her food. He said it would make her meaner. He used to play with her and make her bite stuff like a rope or a towel. He would pull her and lift her off of the ground by her teeth while she was holding on to the towel. Sometimes Bear would bite me or my siblings so hard that she would draw blood. As a reward for biting us or anyone else, accident or not, Eric would go out and buy her a steak and feed it to her raw; of course he would add lots of pepper. Seeing that Enga never objected to Bear's diet, I can only imagine she agreed with his philosophy. Bear used to roam around in the front yard alone. Sometimes people would taunt her through the fence by running back and forth on the sidewalk on the other side of the gate making her bark and chase them. One day a kid was running back and forth at the gate making Bear chase him. When he ran to the end, where the hinged door was, hoping Bear would run into the gate, the gate door burst opened and Bear ran out of the gate and chased him for a short distance. She caught and bit him. I laughed so hard; I thought I was going to bust a gut. Later that day Eric bought her the biggest steak

I had ever seen. People always messed with Bear and we warned them to stop because one day she would get them. That was the last time I remembered anyone ever messing with little Bear.

My sister Kim was constantly in Enga's thoughts and at some point, Enga decided to go back to Boston and steal Kim from Anne. After reaching out to some of her friends and family in the Boston area, Enga found out where Kim was going to school. Her plan was to fly into Boston on a Sunday night, go to Kim's school on Monday morning and simply check her out of school. At that point, she would drive directly to the airport and return to California with only the clothes on Kim's back. Enga bought a round trip ticket for herself and a one-way ticket from Boston to LAX in the name of Kim Crutchfield. With that done, she flew back to Boston. She found a hotel room in a hotel close to the airport and the next day, when she thought Kim should have been in school, she put her plan in motion. Enga took a taxi to Anne's house and put a sealed envelope in her mailbox with just the words "Anne Hill" on it. She then directed the taxi driver to go to Kim's school. Once there, she gave the taxi driver her full fare and an extra $100 bill and said it was his if he would wait for her. Her fare was far less than $100. The driver saw the $100 bill and agreed without hesitation. She went to the front office of the school, presented the women at the front desk with her identification and said she was Kim's mother and was there to check Kim out of school. She made up an excuse that Kim had a doctor's appointment. Enga assured the women that Kim would be back in school the following day. They sent someone to Kim's classroom to bring her to the office. When Kim saw my mother she jumped into my mother's arms hugging her around the neck.

They gathered Kim's things and proceeded out the front door of the school and into the waiting taxi. Enga instructed the driver to head to the airport as quickly as possible, without breaking any laws on the way. While they were in the taxi, having not seen Enga in years, Kim asked Enga excitedly "Where is grandma Anne". Enga told Kim her grandmother had instructed her to pick Kim up and take her on a trip. Kim, now excited, asked where they were going and Enga told her it was a surprise. Now Kim was even more excited, but she asked no more questions. Once at the airport, they boarded the plane and returned to California. When Anne went to her mailbox that afternoon to get her mail, she saw the envelope Enga left her and opened it. Inside was a letter from Enga explaining that she had taken Kim back to California and not to bother looking for her. She explained that there was no way she would allow anyone to take her daughter from her and that she was sorry it took her as long as it did to steal Kim back. She said a number of other things, but in the end, Anne didn't call the authorities. Enga called Anne when she got home to let her know they were safe and actually allowed her to speak with Kim one last time. Her plan went off without a hitch.

Kim soon settled into our family routine. There was an old guy who lived next door to us, known to everyone as Mr. Green. Mr. Green was about 70 years old and was a local Mr. Fix It. He cut our grass in the front and back yards as well as a number of other small projects around the house. I cannot remember if Mr. Green had a wife or family. He always wore green coveralls with suspenders. In addition to his Mr. Fix It duties, he also had a garage in his back yard that he converted into a candy store. He sold a lot of penny candy like individual Reese's cups, Now-and-Laters, Tootsie Rolls, hard candy and small juices and sodas. Mr. Green also built my first bicycle when I was about 5 years old. It was all the same color of brown and all rusted. It had no stickers or designs on it and the pedals matched the rotation of the tires. The faster the wheels rolled, the faster the pedals moved, whether you wanted them to or not. There were no brakes on it. On most bikes you could pedal backwards and the rear wheel would slow or lock up, depending on how hard you pushed. The only way of stopping my bike was to pedal slower. If I pedaled backwards, the bike would go backwards.

When she was an adult, Natasha told Enga that when she was about eight years old, on several occasions, Mr. Green enticed her into his candy store and once there performed oral sex on her and fondle her vagina. In payment for not telling anyone, he gave Natasha as many penny candies as she wanted. Before telling Enga, she never told anyone.

While Mr. Green's candy store may have been an outlet for his enticement of the young girls like my sister, so too was the enticement of the empty field next to our house, to us boys. It was large enough for a house to be built on and it was where we spent most of our days outside. One day we were playing baseball and I was the catcher. I guess I was too close to the batter, because I was in my squatting position waiting for the pitch, the next thing I knew, I woke up in Enga's arms, with a head ache and a black eye. I was told the batter hit me in the head and knocked me out cold. That hit gave him a home run. From then on baseball was not for me.

Although our community was predominantly black and Hispanic, it wasn't unusually violent; small fights would happen here and there. One day I walked in on Aaron and Eric talking about an issue Aaron was having with a kid in the neighborhood.

I recall Eric telling Aaron "I'm not raising no cowards. I'm not raising no bullies either, but I'm definitely not raising no bitches".

With that, he decided that we needed to learn how to defend ourselves. Eric went out and got us some boxing gloves. Aaron and I both got a pair, and Eric got a pair for himself as well. I wondered who Eric would fight. When we got home, Eric called Aaron outside, and immediately Eric got on his knees and started to explain to Aaron how to fight. From time to time, Eric would call Aaron outside and spar with him. At 23 years old, Eric stood 6'2" tall. Even on his knees, he towered over Aaron, who was less than 4 feet tall and very slim. Aaron was not an aggressive person, so being forced to fight an adult presented more than enough challenges for Aaron. Even though Eric was on his knees, his arm length was much longer than Aaron's was. When Aaron went in to swing on Eric he was met with a punch to the face or stomach. It didn't seem like Eric was as interested teaching Aaron how to fight as much as he was interested in teaching Aaron how to take a

19

beating. Aaron never had a chance. I do not recall Eric showing Aaron how to protect himself at all, he just beat Aaron up. They would spar and it looked like Eric would just beat Aaron until he cried. Then at some point Enga would tell Eric to stop and make Aaron come in the house. Every now and then, Aaron and I would spar and I guess Aaron decided to take his frustration out on me because he was always beating me up. At one point he even started to beat me up without the gloves. It got so bad that Eric had to establish some rules. The three basic rules were:

1.   *We could only fight with gloves on*

2.   *If one of us said we were done fighting or didn't want to fight anymore, the   other person had to immediately stop and;*

3.   *These rules didn't apply to Eric*

Aaron beat me up a lot. He beat me up so much that he got really good at it. Therefore, I had decided to stop boxing him. We had stopped boxing for a while, when he asked me to spar again. I initially said no as I didn't want to get beat up which I knew would happen. I reluctantly agreed to fight because he said he would fight me on his knees, in an attempt to even the odds. He was four years older than me, at least a foot taller than I was. The fight began and as usual Aaron immediately

20

started beating me up again, even though he was on his knees. At some point during the fight a neighbor across the street shouted to Aaron and he turned his head to look in the direction of the voice. Just as fast as he turned his head to respond, he turned back to start fighting me again; and with adrenalin pumping my brain, I seized the moment I was waiting for him. I swung at him with every ounce of strength I could muster and hit him in the face hard. When I realized what I had done, I turned and ran towards the house, shaking the gloves off. When I turned to look back Aaron was on my heels and gaining on me. I ran in to the house, through the front room and into the kitchen where Enga was. I ran to her and hugged her around the waist yelling,

"I'm done!! I don't want to fight anymore!"

Like clockwork, she told Aaron to leave me alone. Needless to say, we never boxed again, although he asked often. I often think about that day and it always seems to bring a smile to my face. This incident was a defining moment that characterizes my determined nature to back off from a fight when I'm unprepared.

The community in Compton was friendly, and everyone seemed to look out for each other. Every Christmas, the front room was filled with gifts. Each of the kids seemed to get everything they asked Santa for. Around that time, Eric, made a connection with a drug dealer in Mexico who agreed to provide him with marijuana, lots of marijuana, literally bails of it. They sold marijuana via hand-to-hand transactions, as well as selling wholesale to other dealers. Although they sold marijuana, we didn't experience the violence that is seen among today's drug dealers. Even though I believed everyone in the community knew we sold a lot of marijuana out of our house, our house was never broken into. My parents always had marijuana accessible to them in the common area of the house, and they stored the rest in the attic.

One of the people they sold to was a neighbor across the street named Larry. Even though Larry was the community drug dealer, Larry tried to do good things for the kids in the community. From time to time, Larry would load up his Ford Bronco and take us to Magic Mountain, Disneyland or Knotts Berry Farm. He also rewarded us for picking up trash in the street. If you found litter in the street and Larry happened to be around when you picked it up and put it in the trash, he would give you a dime or sometimes even a quarter. Every year on the Fourth of July, Larry would fill a plastic bag with gasoline and light it on fire. It looked like a monster walking down the street. It was terrifying and we loved it. All the kids in the neighborhood looked forward to it every year.

In addition to the house, Enga used the proceeds of her drug sales to buy a number of things. One of the things she bought was a TransVan. It was only a little larger that a regular van. It had a small kitchen in it, complete with stove and refrigerator; it also had a dinner table that converted to a bed. There was a way of converting the driver's seat and the front passenger's seat into a small bed also. During some summers we would go on a road trip and drive from California to Boston and back, stopping along the way at a number of national attractions. Seeing that it took several days to make the trip, we stopped at night and my siblings slept in a tent outside, while I slept in the front seat bed, and Enga and Eric slept on the dinner table bed.

One night during a trip cross-country, I was awakened by the sound of my mother grunting and then crying. Eric had just hit her and was now yelling at her at a whisper. She begged him to stop and give her a break, almost as if they were taking a lunch break at work, he released her and she lit up a cigarette. Enga must have noticed that I was awake, because she turned to me, pulled the cover up to my chin, tucked me in and told me to go back to sleep. She then patted me as she finished her cigarette while crying. After she finished her cigarette, Eric struck her in her face and started yelling at her again. I heard them fighting for a little while and then she asked for another break.

"No, I just gave you a break!" Eric yelled while continuing to hit her. He was a heartless man when it came to abusing Enga. I was terrified, but didn't know what to do. I ended up falling asleep to her screams and pleas for help.

From time to time Enga's family and friends visited us from Boston. Enga's sister Nicole came when she was on break from Vassar College, pursuing her English degree. She loved spending time with us. Aunty Nicole was a very creative woman; she had ways of keeping us busy. She use to give us tweezers and pay us one penny per hair we plucked from her legs. I rarely got more than three or four. One time my sister Natasha got as many as 18. Life seemed good. On Christmas morning 1977 when I was five years old, Enga decided to introduce us to marijuana. She sat all of us down at the dining room table, lit four marijuana cigarettes and put one in front of each of us, Aaron age nine, Natasha age eight and Kim six years old. She told us it was ours to smoke if we wanted to, but once we started to smoke it we had to finish it. If we got up and walked away, we couldn't come back to it.

Smoking Marijuana was something I saw Enga, Eric and most of my neighbors do daily. They smoked at family gatherings, driving down the street, or just watching TV. It was just a part of everyday life for us. Consequently, I thought it was something I was supposed to do. So, I put it to my mouth, pulled the smoke into my mouth and swallowed. I coughed so hard I thought I was going to see my insides come out of my mouth. I felt horrible, I threw it to the floor and as soon as I could compose myself, I went back to playing with my toys. Kim didn't touch it. Aaron pulled the smoke into his mouth a couple of times and didn't seem to like it. Natasha however liked it. Not only did she smoke all of hers, but she smoked Aaron's, and what was left of mine and all of Kim's. As an adult, Natasha would become addicted to drugs and it would later be her biggest downfall in life.

3

Back to the family business

When I was eight years old, the relationship between Eric and Enga ended. I learned years later that Enga discovered Eric had another woman. A woman who was younger than he was. When Eric left, he took with him the Mexican marijuana connection, leaving Enga with no way of earning money. Unable to pay the mortgage on the house, Enga had a brilliant idea to ask a family friend to burn the house to the ground. As we went away for the weekend to visit family in Oakland, CA, the friend placed a kerosene soaked blanket in the attic of the house and set it ablaze. Unfortunately, only the top portion of the house burned. The contents of the house was soaked with water or damaged by smoke. All of our toys, furniture, beds, dressers, clothes and rugs were destroyed from either the water or smoke.

Instead of the house being deemed a total loss, it was repairable. For three months, we lived in our garage while the insurance repaired the house. After it was fixed, she sold it and we came back to Boston. To this day I wonder why Enga did not just sell the house in the first place. I doubt I will ever get an answer to that question.

When we got settled in Boston, Enga restarted the family business. Unfortunately, as with many prostitutes, she became addicted to cocaine, which eventually led to a crack cocaine addiction. We lived with my maternal grandmother, Matilda who lived in the Mattapan area of Boston. Matilda suffered from paranoid schizophrenia, which was exacerbated by her drinking too much alcohol and being a chain smoker. She had a male friend, Ricky, who stayed with her. Although Ricky was not my grandfather, he was the only grandfather figuratively speaking, that I ever knew. Matilda talked to herself and often when she did, it was out loud and in Spanish a language I never understood. This was a stark contrast to her threats to my mother in her younger days to never speak anything other than 'English'.

Even though I loved my grandmother, I don't think I ever really knew her. With that being said, every time I entered her house, her face lit up like a chandelier and she stopped her conversation with herself to greet, hug and kiss me with sloppy wet kisses I never learned to appreciate. I was definitely her favorite. I was a very shy kid. I was even shy around my grandmother for most of my life. I just never knew how to act around her. Should I interrupt her seemingly important conversation she was always having with herself? When she wasn't talking to herself, she was writing furiously in notebooks, and whatever she was writing seemed really important. She had these notebooks all over the house. Again, my saving grace was Aunty Nicole who would come by often and take us places. Sometimes we went to the movies, and other times, we just hung out with her and her friends.

Not being one to readily open up immediately to people it would take me a while to make any real friends. Aaron however had a number of friends that lived near my grandmother's house. His best friends were Lewis and Russell. They were four years older than me and they rarely allowed me to hang with them. Every now and then Enga would force Aaron to take me with him when they went out. Like most little brothers, I was just a pain in the ass. Russell had recently moved to Boston from Mississippi to live with his father. He did very well in school. He always seemed to be self-motivated in that way. Lewis lived with his mother and sisters next door to Russell. Lewis was always nice to me and seemed to have less of an issue with me hanging around the three of them than Aaron and Russell did. Lewis was the youngest of five children, so he probably understood what I was going through. All three of them were very athletic while I never had an athletic bone in my body. I remember one day we were having a snowball fight in front of Lewis's house. Russell and I were on one side of the street and Aaron and Lewis were on the other. We were both hiding behind mounds of snow and parked cars. We would grab some snow, pack it into a ball, stand up, take aim and throw it at our adversaries across the street. I was holding my own, mostly because all I really did was gather snowballs for Russell to throw while I stayed hidden behind the snow mound. Then as I stood up Lewis released this monster of a snowball and threw it straight at me with all his might. It hit me in the face so hard, I swear the force lifted me off my feet and landed me on my back. All I remember was seeing him throwing it at me, while it seemingly grew larger and larger as it approached my face, then suddenly I felt cold and Russell, Aaron and Lewis were standing over and looking down at me as I looked up from the ground at them. They got me up, made me promise not to tell my mother, and after I agreed, we just went on with our day. Although I usually told Enga everything, I kept that promise and never mentioned it. I figured if they knew I could keep secrets; maybe they would let me hang with them more often. Another trait that has manifested within me and gained me the trust of many to this day.

Back then, we would leave the house and not come back for hours and our parents never came looking for us unless they needed something specific from us. Enga often yelled at us, "Take your butts outside. Get out of this house; I'm tired of looking at you kids". We walked or rode bicycles everywhere. One day, Aaron and Lewis were riding their bikes and an unknown group of kids jumped them in an attempt to get their bikes, Lewis got away unharmed, but they beat Aaron pretty bad. He was bruised all over, his clothes were torn, he was bleeding from the mouth, he had a black eye and worst yet, they took his bike.

Although they remained friends, the relationship between Aaron and Lewis would never be the same. From that point on, Aaron knew that Lewis would not have his back if they needed to defend themselves. Growing up, we were taught that when you leave the house with someone, you come back with them. If the guys got into a fight it was understood that we fought together, unless it was a fair one-on-one situation. Over the years Aaron and Lewis's relationship faded away and as far as I know to this day they still don't speak. As a matter of fact, after that incident, Enga did not want Lewis around anymore. To this very day, she still does not care much for Lewis.

Around this time Enga started dating John, a truck driver who often came to visit us in California. John was about 5'4" tall and 160 pounds and had a lazy eye. Even in his small stature, he towered over the 4'11" Enga. He was a hard worker, and most people who knew John respected him a great deal. Some people were intimidated by him. He was a mechanic, but knew a little about a lot of things and almost always owned his own business. He owned several auto repair shops as well as a junkyard at different times. If I wanted money he was always willing to give it to me as long as I was willing to work for it. I would go to whichever business he had and just hang out doing little things such as handing him a wrench when he asked for it or clean up the shop. However minor the tasks he still wouldn't give me money unless I earned it.

John made sure that even at an early age, I knew what hard work was and if I didn't earn it, I could not have it. Seeing that I never played sports, after school John made me go to his shop and work. It was usually just a couple of hours here and there, but I got used to working. He tried to teach me to be a mechanic, but unfortunately repairing cars never appealed to me, though now I wish I had paid more attention to his lessons. At the time, I liked hanging with John and getting dirt and grease all over myself, but that was as far as my interest in cars went. At one point John owned a junkyard in the Dudley square area of Roxbury. One day after a hard day's work, it started to rain. It rained cats and dogs. It was supposed to rain for a good part of the day, so John got the bright idea that he and I should go to the back of the junk yard and take a shower in the rain water. We put some towels in a plastic bag, got a bar of soap and headed to the back of the junkyard.

We found a place where we were secluded, took off all of our clothes and started to bathe. I thought this was as close to camping, as I wanted to get. Just as we got good and lathered up, the rain stopped. It was as if someone turned off the faucet. We stood there naked with soap covering us head to toe in the back of the junk yard calling for my mother to come and help us. She came back, saw us standing their naked, covered in soap and started laughing at us.

John wasn't amused and instructed her to go and get a bucket of water and come and rinse us off. She went and got a large bucket of water and without warning, threw the bucket of ice-cold water on John. John was furious. What's worse, he still had a lot of soap on him. If I thought he was yelling before, he made sure to show me what yelling was, because he said things a young boy of my age probably shouldn't

32

have heard. Let's just say he was suggesting that my mother should go back and get another bucket of water for us. She went back and got a second bucket of ice-cold water and came and sat it down in front of us and told us to rinse ourselves off. We rinsed off and went to the office. Once there we found Enga on the phone talking to someone and laughing so hard she was in tears.

When I was 13, John took me to a shooting range in Fields Corner section of Boston. He arranged for me to shoot a Walther PPK .380 caliber handgun. He explained to me gun safety and how to hold, aim and shoot the gun. After my brief tutorial, I took the gun, aimed and squeezed the trigger as I was instructed. The bullet hit the paper target close to the center of the target. I kept shooting and found that I was quite the marksman. I loved shooting then, and still do today. John had another family complete with wife and two sons. His oldest son, Jeffrey, was the same age as my brother Aaron and his younger son John Jr. was around my age. I didn't see them much, but we were all friendly. I never met his wife. Jeffrey came to help at the businesses from time to time, but John never did. Jeffrey was friendly and he knew his father and my mother were involved. I often wonder if he told his mother what he knew about us.

When I was about 10 years old, John Jr. and his mother moved out of the state and I never saw him again. Even though we were his "side family" John treated us as much like his family as any man could. I loved him and I knew he loved us. The work ethic I have today is because of John. I tell my kids many of the same things John told me.

4

On the road again

The next few years Enga's addiction had gotten worse. We moved from Boston to Los Angeles and from Los Angeles back to Boston at least three times and to be honest it was not the best situation for children but we adjusted. Sometimes John came with us. When we were in Boston, Aunty Nicole made sure to take us out. She got into skiing, and used to go to Killington, Vermont to ski. She even took me with her and her boyfriend a couple of times. Although I never took to skiing, simply being around the people there showed me a side of the world I never knew existed. Aunty Nicole continued doing things with us like taking us to different places; she tried her best to guide us down what she thought was the right road.

During one of our stays in Boston, Enga sent Aaron and myself to stay with Aunt Ellen. Aunt Ellen was a woman who helped my mother when she was a child. When Enga and Tony would fight, Enga would run to escape Tony's abuse and usually she ran to Aunt Ellen's house making it incredibly easy for Tony to find her. Ellen lived in the Cathedral projects in the south end of Boston. She had a small two-bedroom apartment that she shared with two foster sons, along with her daughter and three young children and various unknown guests. The house was filled with clutter all over and it was infested with cockroaches and mice. There were so many roaches that they would crawl all over the floor, walls and kitchen cabinets. People got so used to them that they rarely killed them. It was almost as if they had as much right to be in the house as we did. It wasn't unusual to fall asleep on the couch and wake up with several strange people sleeping in the front room.

Everyone was friendly and happy to have a place to sleep, but every day, I wished my mother would come back and get me and Aaron out of there. Aaron and I slept on the couch. When we went to sleep, we took our shoes off, and slept in the clothes we already had on. When we got up in the morning, it wasn't uncommon for us to see streams of roaches crawling in, on and around our shoes. I got into the habit of banging my shoes together to get rid of the roaches before I put them on, a habit I still have to this day; even though there are no cockroaches at my house.

One day while in class, another student saw several cockroaches crawling on me. She screamed and drew everyone's attention to me pointing at the roaches. I jumped up and knocked them off of me and stepped on them acting like I had no idea where they came from. To say I was horrified or embarrassed doesn't adequately express my feelings. The kids teased me about that for the rest of the year. Kids can be really cruel. Luckily, we moved around so much that I almost never went to the same school for more than a year.

Unexpectedly, my mother came for us one day because she got us an apartment in the Four-Corners area of Dorchester. That same year, Enga got Aaron and Natasha unique Christmas presents. On Christmas morning Enga went to wake Aaron and Natasha and told them to come into her room and talk to her. Aaron did as he was instructed. When he returned to our room, he started to pack his things. I asked him where he was going. He told me that Enga told him that he and Natasha could no longer stay in our home. Aaron left and ended up sleeping on the floor in Store 24 in Mattapan Square. The next day he came home and apologized to Enga and was welcomed back into the house.

Natasha on the other hand never returned, she was 14 years old. There weren't many ways for a 14-year-old girl to earn a living while being homeless in Boston. She turned to the only business she could think of. What she did not know was that the business she would start was the same business Enga started when she was the same age, "The Family Business". I later learned the reason Enga kicked Natasha out of the house. During that time Enga had begun selling marijuana again, but on a much smaller scale. Enga told me that Natasha stole her marijuana and was selling it at Copley High School and didn't give the profits to Enga. When Enga found out she was furious and since Natasha couldn't be trusted, she had to go.

Around this time, Lewis's sister started to date a guy named Frank. Frank was about 25 years old and seemed to be a ladies' man. I guess that had something to do with their breaking up. After Frank broke up with Lewis's sister, Lewis and Frank became close friends and went everywhere together. Then for some unknown reason Lewis and Frank stopped hanging out and Aaron and Frank got a lot closer. Because Frank was older he was able to get things like alcohol, rent and drive cars. Our parents allowed us to hang out with Frank later at night because he was an adult and they thought he could be trusted. Then at some point Aaron and Frank stopped hanging out and Frank and I became good friends. It never occurred to me to ask why Aaron and Lewis no longer wanted to be friends with Frank. It also never occurred to me or Enga to ask why a 25-year-old man would want to befriend me, a 14-year-old boy or Aaron at 17 years old.

One day Frank and I were hanging out late and we ended up at his house. We were watching TV and there was a power outage, so Frank and I went downstairs to the basement to the fuse box to turn the power back on. After turning the power on, Frank pulled out a small brown glass bottle with a black top. It had a white powder in it. He took some of this powder out and sniffed it, tilted his head back, closed his eyes and stayed there for a few seconds. He asked, "Here, try it". I said no. He explained, "It will make you feel really good." I still refused. He said "You can put it on your tongue and it'll make it numb". I thought that was weird and had felt pressured to try the stuff so I put some on my tongue. Just as he said, it made my tongue numb.

Sometime later, I found myself at Frank's house again after hanging out all day. When it was time to go to sleep, I slept alone in the lower bunk bed in Frank's room. At some point in the middle of the night, I woke up to Frank in the bed with me. He was fondling my penis. When I realized what was going on, I sprung off the bed and exclaimed "I have to go to the bathroom". I went to the bathroom and locked the door and stayed there for hours. When I left the bathroom, it was still dark outside, so I went into the front room and watched TV. As soon as the sun came up, I quietly left the house and walked home, a four to five mile walk. At 14 years old, it seemed like that walk was forever. As I walked, I tried to figure out what happened, why it happened and what was I going to do? While I never thought that Frank could be gay, he obviously was. Do I tell Aaron? Do I tell Enga and John? I decided to keep it to myself and stopped hanging out with Frank.

I became homophobic. At that age, I couldn't process the difference between a man being gay, and one being a pedophile. I convinced myself that every gay guy forced his perversions on defenseless kids before they tried them on adults. I rationalized it by telling myself that all gay men molested defenseless young boys and solidified their sexuality after finding some type of enjoyment from victimizing these children. I would think this way for a very long time. Around this time, I heard that Frank had entered the Navy. I did not know anything about the Navy. I thought everyone in the Navy were out on ships in the ocean and that women weren't allowed on ships, or so I thought.

I imagined that the Navy was where gay men went to serve in the military. I was obviously wrong. A short time later Enga, John,

Aaron, Kim and I moved to Los Angeles. One night while we watched TV, I told Enga and John what happened with Frank. They were furious with me for not telling them when it happened. Even though she was a drug addict, Enga and I had a good relationship, and we talked openly and honestly about almost everything. Somehow I wasn't able to talk to her about this. I was embarrassed, and felt shame. I didn't know if I had done something wrong. I didn't know if this meant I was gay and was just not aware yet. I was afraid of what that might have meant. After telling John, whom I always knew had a gun, he vowed to kill Frank when he saw him, and I believed he would.

5

It's tough in LA

When I was in the eighth grade, we were living in Los Angeles. Those years were the roughest times in my life. Earning money in California was tough for John and this forced Enga to use the welfare money she got from the state which was intended to support us, for her cocaine habit, leaving no money for basic necessities like food or clothes or some of the small things most of my friends had.

Enga signed Kim and me up to attend the Henry Clay Middle School in South Central Los Angeles. Henry Clay was about three miles away from our house. In order to get to school our only option was to walk. Aaron was signed up to go to George Washington School, which was at the corner of our street. Because we had such a long walk, Enga gave us money to go to the mall and get some sneakers. She gave Aaron and me $50 each and we headed to the mall with the biggest smiles on our faces. That was the only time I recalled her giving us money for school clothes.

I walked into the sneaker store and immediately saw these all red Puma's with a black stripe. They were the last pair, and a bonus was that they were my size. I thought they were nice. When I checked the price, I was shocked to learn they were $19.99. All other Puma's were $50 and more. I thought they made a mistake on the price. I asked the salesman how much they cost and he confirmed they were $19.99. I said I'd take them before anyone else bought them.

On the first day of school, I wore my brand new bright red Puma's. My clothes may have been a mess, but my foot gear was on point. A couple of periods into the day, while walking from one class to another, a kid I believed to be in the seventh grade, walked up to me and pulled out a black revolver and pointed it at my stomach. It looked like a cannon in his hands. In retrospect I think it was a .38 caliber revolver. The gun was hidden; only he and I could see it. I thought I was going to die. He said he knew I just moved here from Boston, and told me that if I didn't take these sneakers off my feet, he was going to shoot me. He didn't want them; he just didn't want to see them. I took the sneakers off immediately, put them in my backpack and ran home as fast as my bare feet would carry me.

When I got home, I told Enga what happened. I figured it was a far-gone conclusion that I wasn't going back to that school, so I said the words anyway just to make sure we were in agreement.

43

"I'm never going back to that school!!!" I yelled almost in tears.

"That boy was just warning you", she said as if I was overreacting.

She said it as if what I went through was as minor as getting a splinter in my finger.

"You're gonna be fine", she said.

I thought to myself, 'easy for you to say, you're not the one who almost got killed'. She made me go back to that school, and she was right. I wasn't from the area and didn't understand how the gang situation worked.

At that time, the Crips and Bloods were killing each other left and right and I lived in an area known as "In-Hood Crip" territory, which meant I should be wearing blue. Wearing red meant I was a "Blood" and could have gotten myself killed. That kid probably saved my life. Usually, when people wore red in that school, they were beaten stabbed or shot. No questions were asked as to why they were wearing red, they just pounced on them. Luckily it must have gotten around the school quickly that I was new to California from Boston and didn't understand how the gangs worked. By pulling that gun on me, he showed me how serious the gangs were. Had it not been him, who took pity on me, or had I stayed in school for the full day, I can only imagine what would have happened to me. It certainly would not have been good.

The gangs in Los Angeles were shooting each other daily. If there was a group of people standing on the sidewalk it was common for a car to drive by and randomly fire gunshots at the crowd. This is where the term drive-by shootings originated. To the assailants, it didn't matter whether you were in a gang or not. The simple fact that they did not know you, in their minds, gave them cause to attempt to kill you.

One day one of Aaron's friends approached him with an offer to have him sell cocaine. With no income and not wanting to see his family starve, Aaron brought this idea to my mother. Even though my mother was addicted to the same drug Aaron was about to start selling she knew this drug game was more than he was prepared for. They argued about what Aaron was going to do. Aaron wanted to sell the drugs but my mother knew nothing good would come of it and would only lead him to a life of bad news. She convinced Aaron to decline the offer and he did. The friend and Aaron stopped speaking, as he was furious that Aaron would not assist him in selling his drugs.

During this time we did not have a telephone in the house. Therefore when we needed to call anyone we had to walk about two miles to a pay phone. These pay phones were on the corners of random streets as well as telephone booths in the gas stations. One day my brother went to the telephone booth at a gas station so he could call my aunt to ask her to send us money for food. While in the telephone booth speaking with my aunt, he heard a number of loud bangs and the glass that enclosed the telephone booth shattered. He got down on the ground of the booth as the bangs continued and the glass continued to fall on top of him. When all of the noise stopped he got up and ran home. The shooters were never located and I honestly don't even know if the police looked for them. He was very lucky none of the bullets touched him.

We did not know whether this incident happened as a result of Aaron's refusal to sell drugs or if it was just a random coincidence. A couple of weeks later I was in the shower when I heard several loud booms and the window of the shower exploded. I jumped out of the shower naked and wet. My mother and my sister ran into the bathroom to see what was going on and found me terrified standing in the middle of the bathroom floor butt naked, and dripping wet. Los Angeles was more violent than we could have ever imagined. It was like living in a war zone.

Financially, things were so bad for that entire school year that all we ate at home were oranges. We ate so many oranges that there were no orange oranges left on the tree. Therefore we were forced to eat the yellow oranges. When we had eaten all of the yellow oranges we ate the green ones. Luckily we had an orange tree in our back yard, I don't know what we would have done if that tree wasn't there because it was our only source of consistent food. When we went to school, we filled up on school lunches and snacks. These meals were far from tasty, but we never knew when we would eat again. I grew to love those lunches.

From time to time, Auntie Nicole would send us "Care Packages", with some socks, underwear or t-shirts, or some snacks and various other things from places she visited. Sometimes she even sent us a little cash. During that time, I met Elmore Richmond, who moved to Los Angeles from Florida to live with his father. Elmore's father was a Senior Master Sergeant in the Air Force. Mr. Richmond was a strong black man, intelligent and serious. He didn't talk a lot, but when he did you could tell he thought about what he was going to say before he said it and he meant every word. His wife Rita was about 15 years younger than he was and extraordinarily beautiful. Rita came to the marriage with a daughter named Jordan. Jordan was about two years younger than I was. I developed such a crush on her, but I never had the courage to ask her out. Even if I did ask her out, what would we do? How would I pay for it? They weren't rich, but I figured she would at least want to go to a movie or something and I had no way of paying for it. Their house was meticulous. Even their grass was flawless. Mr. Richmond had converted their garage into a sort of playroom for Elmore and Jordan. The walls in there looked better than the walls in my house; the paint was off white color. It was carpeted, with central air conditioning and a full entertainment center.

This playroom looked better than my house. Mr. Richmond bought Elmore and Jordan a Nintendo game system when Nintendo first came out. Their stereo system was loud and clear. Elmore, Jordan, Kim and I would practice the latest dance moves. Even though I was never good at dancing, I enjoyed hanging out there. I can remember on many occasions Mr. Richmond coming out and even playing "Duck Hunt" with us. Elmore seemed to have it made, and though I thought Mr. Richmond was hard on Elmore; that's not fair, he was firm, yet fair with him. There were many days when I was hungry that my only way of eating was at Elmore's house.

Times were hard, even though I was still a young teen I decided that I would have a better life than what my childhood was. While watching television one day, I saw a commercial for a summer computer program. I told Enga about this program and asked her if I could go. I knew we had no money, but Enga often told me, *"You never know what you can get until you ask"*. A lesson I live with to this day and one that I often repeat to my kids.

Enga agreed to take me to the school and see if she could work it out. When we went to the school, we learned that I was not eligible to attend the school because I was three years shy of 18 years old. The man we spoke with told us that if we came back the next day and my birth certificate said I was 18 years old, he wouldn't question it and he would get me in. On the way home, Enga asked me if I wanted to go to the school, given what we learned. At that point, computers were relatively new and as such, I had no experience with them. I'd seen them in school, and thought they were interesting. I told her I definitely wanted to go to the school.

We went home, and with a pen, she changed the date on my birth certificate, making me 18 years old. The next day she sent me to the school alone to register with this obvious forgery. I found the man we spoke with the day before and presented him with my "new and improved" birth certificate. He brought me into his office, had me sign a bunch of papers and gave me a start date. I went home excited that I had gotten into the program.

On the first day of the program, I noticed that most of the students were older women; I was one of two males in the class. The average age of the students was approximately 30 years old. I quickly learned that this program was designed to teach students to be office secretaries; not exactly what I thought it was going to be about. The curriculum was how to take short hand notes, write business letters, as well as several other office related skills.

The school was far from where we lived, but the school gave me a bus pass as a part of my tuition. Even with the bus pass, it took me almost two hours to get home during rush hour. The man that signed me up for the classes at the school regularly offered me a ride home. I initially said I didn't want a ride and that I did not mind taking the bus. However, at some point I felt pressured and decided to accept his offer. The guy was nice; the problem was that he was too nice. I may have been young, but I had lived and seen enough about life to not be too trusting of adults so quick.

One day for no reason, he started to talk about sexual things he did with women he'd been with. He told me graphic stories of sexual encounters he'd had. He made me very uncomfortable. I was an impressionable 15 year old and had never even kissed a girl. I found the things he said to be simply disgusting. Even though I was attending the school, he knew how old I was. One day, he offered to take me for a ride in the mountains. At that point I got a really weird feeling about him. Not being sure whether he was just being friendly, I decided I wasn't sticking around to find out. When I got home, I told Enga what happened and how I felt about all he had told me.

We agreed that I would never return to the school again and I didn't. At that point I'd only been going there for less than a month. Unfortunately, my decision to attend this school would impact my life for years to come.

6

The beginning of life's harder lessons

Our last move to Boston was in 1989. I was 15 years old and in the ninth grade. One morning my mother woke us up and told us to quietly pack a bag because we were moving back to Boston. We did as we were told and while John slept, we snuck out of the house, went to the Greyhound bus terminal and took a Greyhound bus to Boston. Shortly after arriving in Boston, we moved into a house at 32 Fayston Street in Roxbury and I started going to South Boston High School. At that time, Fayston Street seemed to be the absolute center of the drug universe. Drugs and drug addicts were commonplace. On Fayston Street, it was more unusual to see a person in a suit than it was to see the remnants of used drugs on the street. Once again, I was the new kid in a new school and I didn't know anyone there other than my sister Kim.

One day Enga announced that we were moving back to California to be with John again. Kim and I told her that we did not want to go back. It had only been a few months since we snuck out of the house leaving John without warning to come back to Boston. Even though it wasn't my decision to do that, I was embarrassed to have done it nonetheless. In addition, Kim and I were in school and doing well. Kim had a job as a cashier at Tropical Foods market in Dudley Square, and I was working at a computer technology company called Bachman Information Systems in Kendal Square in Cambridge after school. During the weekends, I worked at McDonald's on Gallivan Blvd in Dorchester. I wasn't making a lot of money, but we were certain we could afford to pay the bills on our own if she left us there. More importantly, we had money to feed ourselves. We had no interest in leaving what we had going on in Boston to go back to California struggling and eating nothing but oranges. My mother had Section 8 and as a result, the rent was minimal. Our jobs just needed to get us enough money to feed ourselves and pay utilities. We were certain we could handle the house expenses if we could convince her to let us stay there. It worked and Enga left us in the Fayston Street apartment and returned to John in California.

I attended South Boston High School. South Boston was a deeply Irish community with a history of racism dating back to the 60's, although now to a much lesser degree, it was very evident then. Feeling vulnerable, I started to carry a pocketknife everywhere I went.

As the year progressed, I made a couple of friends. Natasha came to visit us and brought with her a boyfriend named Will. They visited several times for over a few weeks. One day Will told me he sold guns and asked if I wanted to "be down". At the time I had no friends. If I wasn't at work I was home alone. When Kim wasn't working, she was with her boyfriend. Aaron, Russell and Lewis still didn't want me to hang with them, so wanting to feel a part of something I agreed and told Will that, I wanted to 'be down'.

Will brought me outside to his car, opened the trunk and reached into the area where the spare tire was kept and pulled out a box that looked new. He opened the box right there at his trunk and inside was a Walther PPK .380, the same gun John let me shoot a few years before. Will told me that he was selling this gun in a few hours, but I'd need to carry a gun and have his back if I wanted to be down. I was scared, but not wanting him to know that, I asked him if he wanted me to go with him that night to sell the gun. He said he didn't. I knew getting involved with this was completely wrong and was terrified of going to jail as a result of watching movies about things that happen in jail. Feeling apprehensive I said, "Ok". Will said he would come back the next day with my .380 and he would explain everything I needed to know. Again

I muttered "ok". The next day, I waited and waited for Will, but he never showed up. He never came, as a matter of fact, I never saw Will again. Months later Natasha happened to come by the house and I asked her what was up with Will. She told me that Will was killed in that gun deal that night. God must have been watching over me.

One night while sleeping, I was awakened by something and when I opened my eyes, I saw and felt rats, hundreds of rats crawling all over me. There were so many rats I couldn't see my own skin around them. I began to hit them off of me. I was hitting them hard and I could feel my hand making contact with their muscular little bodies. They hit the floor with a thud and then jumped back on to me. I screamed in horror hoping the sounds would run them off, but it didn't. I kept hitting them off of me, but every time I hit one off, it would jump back on. Then, for no reason, they literally disappeared. I decided to go to the kitchen to get something to drink to wake myself up.

When I opened the refrigerator, I saw large rats inside of the refrigerator eating all of the food. They were in everything. I stared and backed away from the refrigerator in horror. Then seconds later they disappeared again. I didn't know what to do. I was obviously hallucinating. One thing I did know was that I had to be clearly insane.

I wondered if this was the beginning stage of Paranoid Schizophrenia, the condition that my grandmother suffered from. I went back to my room and sat on my bed waiting for the symptoms to get worse. Enga was in California; my sister was at her boyfriend's house, I didn't know what to do, so I stayed in my bed on guard. As a result of that incident, I was petrified of rodents. I remain that way to this very day. It would be years before I told anyone about this hallucination, and even then, I never sought counseling to attempt to understand what happened and why.

7

Life's Pivotal Moments

Later that year, while in school, a guy named Steve approached me and said some kids were planning to jump him and asked to hold my knife. He knew I carried a knife for protection. It wasn't uncommon for people to carry knives. I initially said no, but he talked me into giving it to him, so I did and then went to my next class. Less than half way through the class the principal knocked on my class room's door and instructed me to get all my things together to come and talk with him in the hall way. When I got in the hallway, Steve and the principal were standing there. The principal produced the knife I gave Steve and asked me if it was mine. I said it was. Apparently, as soon as Steve left me, he managed to get himself caught with the knife. When they asked him where he got the knife from he told them it was mine. He was so helpful to the principal that he gave them my full name and told them exactly where to find me. We were both suspended and ordered to go to a special school for two additional weeks called the *Barron Center*.

The Barron Center was for kids who showed a propensity for violence. A bus picked me up in the morning from my house and brought me to the Barron Center. From the front, The Barron Center looked like a regular brick building on Washington Street in Roslindale. In the rear, it was fenced in. Although I carried a knife, I wasn't a bad kid. I wasn't the kind of kid that misbehaved, or went looking for trouble. I carried the knife for protection, nothing more. Some of the kids at the Barron Center really needed to be there, I didn't. The Barron Center wasn't focused on education as much as it was on correcting the thought process of at-risk youths. They took us on field trips, they had speakers come in and show us a number of films they figured would make a difference. After school, the bus dropped me off at my front door and waited for me to go in.

One day the Barron Center took us on a field trip to the Charles Street Jail. As soon as we entered the jail and completed some paperwork, they brought us to an area of the jail where there were some empty cells and instructed each of us to enter our own cell. After we entered the cell, the staff made a small speech and said that this is where we're going to end up if we didn't start to make better choices. Then they left the area and closed the door behind them leaving each of us in our individual cells. They left us there alone for about an hour. Then the door swung open and I heard a loud voice yelling, "Anthony

Crutchfield!!!!" It was a deep male voice and he was obviously angry about something. I hadn't done anything to my knowledge.

The voice repeated, "Anthony Crutchfield!!!"

"Yes sir", I said in what must have sounded like a mouse squeaking.

"Anthony Crutchfield, sound off. Where are you", the voice said.

I squeaked again, "Here sir".

He came to my cell and stood there looking at me for a little while. He was huge. He reminded me of my stepfather's friend "Niggaplease". He was about 6'3" and around 300 pounds of solid muscle. Even his muscle's had muscles.

He announced, "Your father is Anthony Crutchfield."

I shook my head in agreement.

"Your mother is Enga."

Again I nodded my head.

"You have a cousin named Troy and an uncle named Cuso."

Again he was correct and I was afraid to ask how he knew, as this information wasn't included in my paperwork. I did not have to ask because he answered my unasked question.

"I know your entire family." He said as he stood there staring at me.

He went on to say, "I'll see you in here", as he turned and started to walk away.

"No sir", I squeaked.

He stopped in his tracks, turned and rushed back to me like he was going to blow through the cell door like a white-hot knife through warm butter. I'd never been so happy to be in a jail cell in my life. The cell was the only thing keeping him from ripping my head off.

He then said, "What did you say, say it again!?"

"I just said, No sir, you won't see me in here"

"I'll see you in here, you Crutchfield's are STUPID. Every last one of you Crutchfield's are STUPID!!" He said as spit came out of his mouth. "You don't have a choice; it's in your blood. You're gonna follow in your father's footsteps and I'll be kicking your ass for years just like I did your father."

I was frozen with fear, and couldn't respond. With nothing more to be said, he walked away. I vowed to myself to never see the inside of a jail cell again. I was successfully "scared straight".

At some point Enga came back from California again and moved back into our apartment and life went on. Seeing that her section 8 was paying our rent, we had no authority to stop her from moving back in

60

with us. When I was 17 years old and a senior in high school, Aunty Nicole was an English teacher at Latin School in Boston. After school, I went and hung out at her school. There were a lot of pretty girls at Latin School, so going over there wasn't a chore. I made some friends and I started to date one of her previous students named Jessica. Although Aunty Nicole didn't express her opinion on Jessica, no one else in my family liked her. It was at this point I developed a plan to better my life. I thought about Mr. Richmond and made a plan to join the military, hoping I would end up as he did. After hearing family and friends tell me things like, "The black man has no place in the army?" and "why you want to die for this country, what has it done for you?"

I was torn, but seeing what my options looked like so far, I decided to enlist. The first Gulf war had just started and then Jessica told me she was pregnant. She asked me what I wanted her to do. I told Jessica that what she did was completely up to her. My decision in that matter ended at the moment she became pregnant. I told her it was her body and I would respect whatever she decided, but whether she had the baby or not, I was not leaving her. Jessica decided to have the baby. To Jessica, having the baby meant she could get welfare and be able to leave her mother's house. Shortly after telling her mother about the pregnancy, her mother kicked her out of the house, and Jessica went to live at her father's house. Although Jessica's father, Ernest, seemed to be a nice guy, when he was angry, he would physically and emotionally abuse Jessica. When Jessica was nine months pregnant Enga knowing that Jessica was not happy at home, asked her to move in with us. Jessica agreed and moved in shortly after. While we waited for the birth of the baby, people often asked what we thought the sex was going to be. I wanted a boy. I had convinced myself that I was going to have a boy and I was going to name him "Troy Anthony Crutchfield". I'd had the name picked out for years.

One day, Auntie Nicole and I were talking and I told her I was certain that I was having a boy, and Auntie was equally certain that I was having a girl. We made a bet on it, Auntie had a Blue Toyota Corolla Lift-Back she named Frances. The deal was that if I had a girl, I would name the baby after Auntie's car. I convinced Jessica to agree with me. Soon after, Jessica went into labor. When the baby first came out I saw a slight bulge and yelled out, "It's a boy!!" I was wrong. Jessica gave birth to a beautiful baby girl. We kept our promise and named her Frances. Unfortunately, I had never even thought about the possibility of us having a girl.

Therefore, I didn't do any research on the name "Francis" being the male version, or "Frances" being the female version. A woman came to our room shortly after the birth and asked us for the name of the baby. Jessica was still heavily medicated and barely conscious, so the woman handed me the paper to write down the name of the baby. I wrote down 'Francis', not knowing that this was the male spelling of the name. We never attempted to correct my error.

I was determined to do what I thought was the right thing, I dropped out of high school, stopped my attempt to enter the military and got a full time job working with Aaron as a delivery driver for a copy shop in Harvard Square called Gnomon Copy. One day after work, Aaron gave me a ride home. When we arrived in front of my house on Ashmont Street in Dorchester, there was a taxi that slowed directly in front of us. It stopped in front of my house and Jessica's father Ernest exited the back. Ernest never came to my house, so I knew something was wrong. Jessica opened the door for me. As soon as I saw Jessica, I said,

"What's wrong?"

"Our parents want to talk to us." She said

"About what?"

"I have no idea", she responded.

I said, "Okay"

I went upstairs and found Enga and Ernest waiting for us in the front room. Ernest started talking and Enga was silent. At the end of Ernest's speech he said he had become a very religious man and could no longer accept Jessica and me living together in sin. He went on to say that he and Enga decided that Jessica and I should get married. Jessica and I had spoken about marriage, but we hadn't decided to actually do it on a specific date. He said that we must file for a marriage license and get married by the next week. I explained to Ernest that only one person would decide when and who I married and that person was me. He responded by saying that I didn't have a choice. He then looked at Enga for her to say something to us since it was apparent that they were in agreement. Enga then stated that seeing that Ernest had these issues, Jessica and I should get married or we would have to move out of the house. Jessica was silent. I repeated to her again, I wasn't ready to get married and I had no place to go. I told her if she wanted me to leave I would, but whatever happened after this meeting, it wouldn't end with me getting married until I was ready and at that moment I simply wasn't. She said in that case I needed to pack my stuff and get out. I said OK, thinking she would stop me at some point. She didn't. I called Aaron and asked if I could move in with him and his girlfriend. He said I was welcome to stay that night, but by the next day I needed to figure out a place for us to stay, but I couldn't live with him.

I had heard through the grapevine that Natasha had recently gotten an apartment; the problem is that she was addicted to crack and prostituted herself to support her crack addiction. I didn't have any other option, so I called her. I told her what had happened and she agreed to not only allow us to move in, but she actually gave us her bedroom, while she slept on the couch. She said she wouldn't even charge us rent. We moved in and I worked and saved every penny I could.

About two weeks after being there, Tony, who was a pimp, and one of his prostitutes came for a visit. We talked and told stories for hours. That night when I went to bed, everyone was still up talking. I had to work in the morning, so regretfully I had to get some rest. I was truly enjoying my first real visit in a while with my father. When I woke up, Tony and his girl were sleeping on the floor in the front room, Natasha was on the couch. I went to work and left Jessica and Francis at the house. When I returned, Tony and his girlfriend were still there.

A week later, they were still there. His girl would go and work in the early evening and come back after I was asleep.

Natasha was using crack cocaine and people were in and out of the house all day and night. One night Natasha called me into the bathroom and showed me a used hypodermic needle on the bathroom sink. She said it was Tony's. We suspected he was still using heroin, but we didn't know for sure. We both knew he had already been diagnosed with the AIDS virus. We were both furious at him for taking the chance of infecting us with this horrible disease.

Natasha told me that since I was the man of the house it was my responsibility to inform him that he was no longer welcomed there. My heart almost jumped out of my chest. I was 17 years old and this wasn't even my house. I'd had minimal contact with Tony and had no idea how he would respond to me telling him that he could no longer stay there. I appreciated Natasha taking us in, and didn't want to make her angry by refusing. A little while later when Tony returned to the house I asked to speak to him outside. I explained to him that Natasha and I saw a needle in the bathroom sink and Natasha told me that I had to ask him to leave. Surprisingly, he was very understanding. He said he knew it was hard for me to approach him with this, and wouldn't make the situation any more difficult than it already was for me. He agreed to leave and did so that night. I appreciated his understanding. By the end of the month, Jessica found us an apartment; all we needed was first and last month's rent, which I successfully had as a result of all the hours I was putting in at Gnomon Copy.

The apartment was on East Springfield Street, near Boston City Hospital in Roxbury. Things were finally going well, or so I thought. I was certain that I wanted Francis to have a better life than I had growing up. I decided I had to be a better parent to Francis than my parents were to me. Because of Aunty Nicole, I knew education was the key, but going back to school wasn't an option for me because I had to keep working full-time in order to support us. However, I decided to get my GED. The problem was that I never did well in school; I was a solid C-student. I had heard that people took the test and failed it many times. Regardless, I arranged to take the test and I passed it on my first attempt. I guess I was a better student that I gave myself credit for.

One day after work, Jessica told me that she wanted to see other people. She said she was lonely and she never saw me because I was always working. I wasn't making a lot of money but took my responsibility to support my family seriously. Therefore, I worked a lot.

I couldn't imagine my life without Francis, and didn't want her to grow up without me. Therefore, I agreed to have an open relationship, under the condition that the people we dated didn't come to or call the house. I was working at the copy shop six days a week from open to close. Even though I had a baby, I was still very shy. I didn't have time to find another girlfriend. I hoped that Jessica would soon realize what she had in me and we would make it through this bump in the road.

One day after work, my phone rang. I picked up the receiver and said "Hello". A male voice on the other end said, "Let me speak with Jessica". I asked who it was and he told me his name. I hung up the phone and went to discuss the situation with Jessica. We had a huge fight and I moved out that night, but we agreed I could see Francis every weekend I wasn't working. I moved in with my childhood friend Russell. Russell was finishing up his Bachelor's degree in Mechanical Engineering at Boston University. Russell and I became great friends.

When I was 19 years old, Russell got me a job at a video store in Brookline called Beacon Video. Russell, a college student, was building his credit and suggested that I did the same. He explained that I would need credit for the rest of my life. So, since I had a stable job, I applied for my first credit card. I was denied. I couldn't figure out why I got denied. Later I applied for a different credit card that I was told should be easy to get, and again was denied. I got a copy of my credit report and discovered that when Enga had changed the date of birth on my birth certificate to get me into the school in California years before, the papers I signed were loan papers. My credit report indicated that I had a student loan in default for more than $18,000.00. Russell suggested I start making payments in order to get it out of default. I didn't follow his advice. I tried to get credit many times over the next few years and each time I was usually denied. When I was finally granted credit, the interest rate was unreasonably high. I knew nothing about credit or how it worked.

Because I was frustrated that all my friends had credit cards and I couldn't get one. I wrote a letter to the holder of my defaulted student loan explaining what had happened. They instructed me to send them proof of my claim, specifically an original birth certificate. After sending them the information they requested to prove that I wasn't eligible for the loan when I got it, they removed the fraudulent entry from my credit report. By that time I had developed such poor habits around credit it took me years to get my credit back on track. In the meantime, a new video store opened in Somerville called Palmer Video and Russell asked me if I wanted to work there as well. I said yes, and soon after I was working at both video stores.

Palmer Video Store was connected to a Walgreens Pharmacy. One day, while working at the video store, I went into Walgreens with the intention of getting some ice cream. As I walked to the freezer area, I looked down one of the aisles and noticed an employee doing something on the lower shelf. She had a caramel complexion, long hair. She wore thick glasses, was slim and had a body to die for. She had small, but perky breasts. Her waist was small, but her butt was large and shapely. She was perfectly proportioned. Again, I was shy, so I didn't have the courage to approach her and ask her name, but I knew I liked her. I got my ice cream and went back to work. When I got back to the video store, I said to a co-worker, "I just met my wife!"

I later became an assistant manager at Palmer Video. The video store was small, and sometimes the general manager didn't get enough change for us to last the weekend and I was forced to go to the Walgreens manager to get change for our customers. One of the manager's, Steve and I became very friendly. One day I shared my interest in the girl and learned her name was Gilda. I asked Steve to see if she was single and if he could find out if she had any interest in going on a date with me. I asked Steve to give her my phone number. To ensure she got me when she called, I gave Steve my home phone number, the phone numbers to both the video stores and my pager number. I wanted to make sure I didn't miss her call. Steve reported back to me that she said to tell me that if I was interested in her to talk to her myself. I was terrified. I had a child, but I'd never actually approached a girl and tried to pick her up. I had no idea what to say if I got up the courage to approach her. I liked her and it took me a couple of weeks to finally approach her. When I did, I asked her to go to a movie with me and she agreed without hesitation.

I wanted to make a good impression on her, so I asked Frank, if I could borrow his car to take her out. His car was an older model bright yellow Chevy four-door, about 15 years old and didn't run well. I figured it was better than taking the bus to the movies. When I arrived at her house my heart was beating so hard I thought it was going to jump out of my chest. This girl was unbelievably beautiful and I figured at some point she was going to change her mind about going out with me, but until she did I was going to do everything I could to make her have a great night. I got to her house early, and sat up the street debating with myself about how early I should pick her up. If I went too early I'd seem desperate, if I was late, it would look like I didn't respect her time. I finally decided to ring her doorbell 15 minutes before I told her I'd be there. Surprisingly, she was ready. When she came down stairs, she was wearing a pair of blue jeans and a green top. I don't remember much about the top she wore, because all I could focus on was her lower half. I was never really an ass man, but I was from this moment on. I could describe her lower half, but let's just say it was absolutely perfect. With that said, let's move on…

I made sure to walk her to the car, open the passenger door for her, and assist her in getting in the car. It was overkill, but I was a gentlemen and I wanted her to know it. I ran around the car to the driver's side still unsure the date was going to happen. When she didn't get out of the car, I decided to drive towards the Showcase Cinemas Revere Movie Theater until she said different. I couldn't imagine a girl that looked like her being interested in me. I decided that we would see a movie called A Few Good Men starring Tom Cruise and Demi Moore. I spared no expense. We got popcorn, candy and a drink for each of us. We went in, found some seats and started watching the movie. Now at some point, I knew I had to show her affection, but I didn't want her to think I was being too forward. About half way through the movie I decided to try to hold her hand. I decided to make my move and she didn't resist it either. I was on cloud nine. I held her hand for a while and decided to make THE MOVE... I reached up pretending to stretch and put my arm around her shoulders and she leaned forward allowing me access, then she did it. She leaned in and kissed me on the mouth!! I don't have the words to express my feelings at that moment.

After a while I became uncomfortable with my arm around her. Then my arm started to get that tingling feeling. There was no way I was going to remove my arm from her shoulder though. Then, just at the moment that I didn't think I could take the pain anymore, my pager went off. I looked at it and recognized Frank's phone number. I told Gilda that Frank paged me and I was going to go to the pay phone and call him. She said she'd come with me. When we got to the pay phone, I called the number in my phone and as the phone rang, she kissed me again!! It was Frank on the other end of the phone. He needed his car as soon as possible. I told him I'd leave the movie immediately, drop Gilda off and head his way. On the way to her house, we stopped at a red light and she leaned in and kissed me again. Even as I write this now, I am unable to express the excitement that went through my body. I took her home, and we talked about going to see Bobby Brown in concert over in Worcester a couple of weeks later. She volunteered to buy us the tickets. I was in shock because I had planned on doing it since it was my suggestion. Three days later we got hit with a huge snowstorm.

It was the largest snowstorm since the blizzard of '78. I was working at Palmer Video and before I could get out of work the public bus system shut down. I was stuck. Gilda was next door at Walgreens, but she lived within walking distance. She lived with her parents', her two sisters who were ages 15 and 10 years old and her brother who was 26 years old and in college. Gilda suggested that I stay at her house. I hadn't met her parents when we went to the movies, so I was certain that they wouldn't allow that. Gilda clarified "You'd be sleeping on the couch". I laughed and suggested that she ask her parents first. She called back a short time later and said they had agreed. After work, we walked to her house. When we got there, her 55 and 65-year-old parents were shoveling the snow in front of the house. I asked her mother for her shovel and started shoveling. After shoveling for a while, we went inside and her mother had the downstairs couch already made up for me.

I had never even met her parents and here they were allowing me to sleep in their house. They were both very pleasant, but being from Haiti, they spoke Creole and very little English. They welcomed me in their home with open arms that night and any other night I wanted to borrow their couch.

After working at Palmer Video for about 18 months, I quit and got a job as a special police officer at New World Security, patrolling low-income housing developments in Boston. After completing a 160-hour training program, I was assigned to patrol on foot as well as in a vehicle, enforcing the laws of the Commonwealth of Massachusetts.

A regular police officer's training program is about 1040 hours. In the capacity of a special police officer, I made numerous arrests for crimes such as possession of drugs, distribution of drugs and possession of firearms, although I found an unusual pleasure in making drug arrests, I also made arrests for incidences such as disturbing the peace, domestic violence, assault and battery, and various other crimes. Unfortunately, not all of the people I worked with should have been in law enforcement. While working at New World, I learned that when given positions of authority some people abuse it. Most officers at New World Security tried to do the right thing, but others would simply abuse their authority and wrongfully took people's freedom away. During this period of my life I became aware of the impact that this authority can have in changing people's lives.

Russell had graduated college and was working for a robotics company called PRI, which required him to travel the world repairing these machines. Even though he had a good job, he and I continued to work at Beacon Video, part-time. Russell and I were like brothers. One day Russell came to me and told me he and the owner of Beacon Video had discussed Russell buying the video store. Russell knew I couldn't afford to put money in with him towards the purchase of the store. Therefore he made me an offer. His suggestion was that if I agreed to work at Beacon Video from open to close on the weekends without pay for one full year; at the conclusion of that year, he would consider me an equal partner.

I said, "Deal" without a thought. I wasn't supposed to start this arrangement until he purchased the video store. We didn't put this agreement in writing, because we were brothers, in some ways more brothers than our own brothers. We always looked out for each other, even though it was usually Russell who taught me about life's lessons, and we simply didn't think of it. A couple of months later Russell's robotics job sent him to Italy for four months to work on their machines. Even though he was thousands of miles away, we stayed in constant contact and he gave me assignments to handle at Beacon Video. One day he gave me an important assignment to handle during my shift.

Unfortunately, at the same time Francis needed to go to the hospital, which caused me to have to get someone else to work at Beacon in my place. During the following week, Russell called to get the status of the assignment he'd given me. When I told him I hadn't done what he'd asked, he was furious. I explained why I wasn't at work and he simply didn't care. He started yelling at me and we got into a rather heated argument. I attempted to explain to him why I didn't complete the assignment in several ways, but he couldn't seem to get my point. Therefore in a moment of frustration, I said,
"If I ever have to choose between Beacon Video and Francis, "Fuck Beacon!!!""
With that said, we wrapped up the conversation and I told him I would complete the assignment during my next shift, and I did. Russell returned home a couple of weeks later. At the following monthly employee meeting, he opened the meeting stating, "As of yesterday, I am the President", as he slammed documents on the counter. "I am the

77

Vice President", slamming down more documents. "I am the Secretary and I am the Treasurer of Beacon Video, Beacon Video is mine".

After the meeting I pulled him aside and asked him what this new ownership meant for me? He said,

"It means Beacon Video is mine".

He went on to say, "Do you remember when you said if you had to choose between Beacon Video and Francis, "F" Beacon Video?" I remembered saying it. I meant it when I said it and I still meant it. Beacon Video was a small business. Worst-case scenario, we would lose a day or two of income. Even if the store shut down, how could anyone expect me to put the well-being of a video store over the well-being of my daughter? Francis was still an infant of maybe three years old.

"Yeah I remember." I said.

Russell immediately responded "Then "F" Beacon. By saying that, you were saying you didn't want to be a part of owning the store". That wasn't what I meant and he knew it. I felt like he used me to work open to close for months while dangling partnership in front of my face. I was furious. I didn't see the point in arguing about it.

I said "okay" and let it go. The lesson I believe that has stayed with me throughout my life from this incident was to be clear when making decisions, no matter how simple the issue.

One day I got an unexpected call from my sister Natasha, who I had not spoken to in years. I had heard that she was still addicted to crack cocaine, so I kept my distance. She told me that after fighting Social Security for several years in an attempt to get benefits, she was finally approved. Because she was an addict, Social Security wouldn't pay her the money directly; she needed a payee. A payee was someone to receive Social Security payments on behalf of this person who in this case couldn't be trusted with the money. The payee would then pay the intended recipients bills. She said because she applied a number of years ago, she would be receiving payments that were retroactive from the day she was approved. Therefore, her first check was going to be for over $10,000.00. She went on to say that she initially asked Aaron to be her payee. Aaron said he would be her payee but he wanted to use her money as a down payment on a house. Natasha said she didn't want to buy a house and seeing where Aaron's head was, she no longer wanted him to have control of her money. She then asked me to be her payee. I was hesitant, but I wanted to establish a relationship with my sister.

Therefore, I agreed. Although she and I didn't speak regularly, I appreciated the fact that she was there for me when I needed her years before.

One day I went to my mailbox and found two checks totaling approximately $10,000.00 for Natasha. I took the checks to work with me and cashed them on the way. After work I went to Natasha's house and showed her the cash. Natasha was living in a small one-bedroom apartment on Normandy Street in Roxbury. Her house had no furniture. I told Natasha I was off the next day and would come by, pick her up and take her shopping and furnish her apartment. She immediately asked for some money so I felt the need to lay down some ground rules. I told her that Social Security informed me that I was responsible for the money and needed to have receipts for all purchases. They said they would understand if I gave Natasha cash from time to time, but for the most part, the money needed to be accounted for. I told her I would give her $50.00 right then and asked that she have some of the money when I came to get her in the morning. At that point it was midnight. The next morning around ten o'clock, Gilda and I went to her house since I had promised to take her shopping. I asked her if she had any of the money I gave her 10 hours ago and she said she was broke. I knew then

80

she couldn't be trusted with cash, but I loved her and wanted her to be happy. We first went shopping for a bedroom set as she was literally sleeping on the floor. After choosing a reasonably priced set, we went and got a kitchen table and chairs. We then got her a full front room set that included a couch, love seat, coffee table, end tables, lamps, TV and TV stand. We got some things for her bathroom and then went food shopping.

I spent more money in that one day then I ever spent in my lifetime to that point. I made sure to keep all receipts, including the one for groceries. I also gave Natasha $50 more and told her that I would give her $100 in cash weekly. I went on to tell her, she wouldn't get any more money from me unless I felt it was an emergency.

Surprisingly, the next day, she had an emergency and needed more money. I refused. She begged and begged and I refused. She called Enga and they both called me on three-way and Enga convinced me to give her another $50. I told them both that I would give her $50 more, but after that, I didn't care what happened and I meant it. Natasha wouldn't get any more money from me until the following week. I wasn't too surprised that the next day, Natasha had another emergency. I told her that not only would I not give her any more money, even if

Jesus Christ himself came down and asked, I'd tell him NO. She could feel free to call anyone she wanted; she wouldn't get any more money from me until she was scheduled. She said she was going to call Social Security and tell them I stole her money. I told her to call anyone she wanted and tell them anything she wanted. I didn't think she would actually risk getting me in trouble seeing that I was just trying to help her. Boy was I wrong.

Sometime the next week, after I gave Natasha her allowance, I got a letter from Social Security telling me an allegation had been made against me and I needed to come into the office with all receipts and account for the money. I got the receipts together along with a money order for the remaining balance and went to the Social Security office. I gave them the receipts and explained to them how much money I gave Natasha in cash and I also gave them the money order and instructed them to remove me as her payee. That night Natasha called and said she needed more money. When I told her about my meeting with Social Security, I also told her I gave Social Security all the receipts and cash I had left over. She burst into tears saying it would take her months to get her money, now that it was back in the system. I told her I didn't care, and instructed her to never call me again. One day while I was working at Beacon Video, Tony walked in. I didn't know he knew where I worked. We hadn't been in contact for years and even when we were, he never knew where I worked, or so I thought. We made eye contact and he went to the back of the store and patiently waited until I had finished with the customers. After the store was clear of customers he approached me and said "Hey son, we've got a problem". I asked what was up and he informed me that Natasha was holding some drugs and money for a member of the "Intervale" street gang.

In those days, the Intervale gang was one of the most violent gangs in the City of Boston. They were rumored to be responsible for not only drug sales in the area, but murders, assaults and robberies as well. When this gang member came to get his drugs and money, Natasha told him I came to her house, put a gun to her head and took his drugs and money. It was obviously a lie. She went on to give him a picture of me and told him where I worked and that I walked around in the community all the time. In essence, she tried to have me killed. Tony told me not to worry about it; he would take care of it. I never heard anything more about it.

8

Gilda

The relationship I had with Gilda grew daily. She became more than my girlfriend, she became my best friend. When I did things wrong, she was always able to correct me in a way that didn't make me feel attacked or berated. Anytime we weren't working or she wasn't in school, at Bunker Hill Community College, we were together. Although she hadn't met my family, I met all of her immediate family and quite a bit of her distant family. They all loved me and I loved them. Her parents treated me like I was their natural born son. When it snowed, I made sure I slept on their couch so I could help shovel in the morning. When my car needed tires, her father bought me a set of four. When their family car broke down, I found someone to fix it at a cheap price while doing good work. When her father went looking for a new car he waited until I was available and when we got to the dealership, he introduced me as his son and Gilda as my girlfriend. Gilda reminds both him and me of that to this day.

One day Gilda and I were out shopping for a gift for her sister Sandra's 16th birthday. We were downtown Boston and Gilda decided

84

on getting Sandra a ring. After shopping around at several jewelers, Gilda and I went into one last place. Luckily she found the ring that she thought Sandra would like. As the Jeweler went over the details of the ring including description of the gem and cost, I went outside. When she came out, she had a bag with two small boxes inside. She took one box out and handed me the bag. Before we could even get to the corner, she said,

"I got you something", as she handed me the other box.

Feeling weird I looked at her and didn't know what to say. It wasn't my birthday or any other occasion that would warrant a gift.

"Open it" she said.

I handed her the bag and opened the box. Inside I found a gold ring with an onyx stripe going from one side to the other. On one side of the onyx were two small diamonds that were close together. She said the onyx line was the line that no one could get across to reach our hearts, which were represented by the diamonds.

She then said, "Will You Marry Me?"

I immediately said "yes!"

I didn't know how this was supposed to go. I didn't know what I should be looking for in a wife. What I did know was that I'd never loved a woman as much as I loved her and I didn't want to imagine my life without her. When I thought about what I should be looking for in a wife, I figured it should be someone I loved, someone who was supportive, someone who's family I loved and most importantly, my BEST FRIEND. It was 1994 and we were a young 23 years old, but I couldn't imagine being more compatible with someone else.

With that being said, I wasn't in a rush to take the walk down the aisle either, and I wanted to make sure we had her parents' approval. A short time after this, Gilda called me from work and said her mother wanted to know if I would drive her to the Watertown mall. I said of course and headed to their house. Seeing that her parents went almost everywhere together, I assumed that Gilda meant her mother, father and sister.

When I got there, I rang the doorbell and her mother; Violetta came down with her purse ready to go, but this time she was by herself. We walked to the car and I opened her car door and assisted her with getting in- as I usually did. I ran around to the driver's side jumped in the car and drove to the mall. We walked around the mall looking for the things she needed and then I said,

"Mom can we sit down and talk for a minute?"

She said, "Sure", and we found a bench.

I said, "I love Gilda and I know she loves me too. I'd like your permission to ask her to marry me."

She looked at me then smiled and laughed. At that point I got really nervous. I stayed silent and waited for the punch line. When she stopped laughing, she got quiet, looked me in the eye, shook her head and said, "Shouldn't you be asking Clement this question?"

I shrugged my shoulders, as I was truly confused.

Then she said, "OK, do you already have the ring?"

"No". I shamefully replied.

She started looking around, got up and started to walk away. Confused, I got up and followed her.

Being from Haiti, English was her second language, but she spoke English a million times better than I spoke Creole. I thought I missed something. As we walked I asked where we were going but she didn't say anything, so I just followed and figured I'd find out shortly.

She walked to a jewelry store and went right to the engagement ring section. We sat there and looked at rings and talked about what she thought Gilda would like. She said there is no need to be in a rush to get something. I told her my plan was to take my time and get what I could afford that I thought Gilda would like. We left the mall, and I brought her back to the house.

By October of 1995 I had gotten Gilda a ring and we were at Nicole's house discussing the wedding that we had loosely started to plan. Although we had not settled on a date, we, (meaning Gilda, her sister and her mother), were getting things we would need regardless of when the wedding was.

At that point it occurred to me that that coming February was a leap year. So, being a smartass, I said we're getting married on February 29. That way I would only get in trouble once every four years for forgetting my anniversary. I was serious, but not really serious. Gilda was surprised seeing that we had not even discussed it together. With that said, she also wasn't going to argue about it and at that second she shifted her plans into high gear.

When we got back to her house she told her mother what I said. They went to the church where Gilda was baptized and did her first communion, found the priest that baptized her, told him our plans and asked him to marry us, he agreed. He told them that the church was already booked that night. Someone had stolen my idea. Either way,

Violetta wasn't crazy about having the wedding on a Thursday night either way.

Hearing that my date was taken, Gilda called and told me that her mother wanted us to get married on that following Saturday. I agreed and we were married on March 2, 1996.

9

Toni

Gilda had a large family and it was not unusual that she would want to have several children. I on the other hand loved children, but never really felt secure with my ability to care for my family. I think the things I saw and experienced growing up made me very cautious about planning a family. I knew that as a husband and father, I would be responsible for much and I wanted to do a great job. What I also knew was that I had no intention to have a family that was larger than I could afford to support. I refused to allow my children to have the type of upbringing I had. At the time I was working at New World Security and had no benefits and every year I anxiously hoped the company kept the security contract or I would be out of a job. Gilda's position was that we would never be completely ready for a child but as long as we loved each other and worked hard together we would make it work.

After discussing it for a couple of years, we decided to have a child. Gilda became pregnant in 1998. At that time Gil, Francis and I were living with Russell in a 2-bedroom apartment in East Boston. When Gilda became pregnant, we told Russell who had always supported me. Russell told me that he had been thinking about buying a house. He went on to say that he would move up his schedule and buy a house leaving the apartment to Gilda and me. For months Russell looked and in October he came to me and informed me that he couldn't find a house to buy and as a result he was not moving out of the apartment. In addition, he said his home was too small for five people so Gilda and I had to move. At this point Gilda was eight months pregnant. I told him it was going to be incredibly difficult for us to find an apartment in less than a month.

He informed me to do what I had to do, but he did not want to live with four people including our child when it was born. We were living check to check, and hadn't been saving. Therefore we didn't have first, last and security deposit most renters required. I went to work and told Shelton, a coworker who was in the process of purchasing a three family house on Draper Street in Dorchester, the challenge I was facing at home. Shelton told me he was buying the house with his sister. Their plan was for each of them to take an apartment and rent out the first floor. He said because we were friends and I was between a rock and a hard place, I could have the house and I didn't need to have last month's rent or the security deposit. He said the house needed work, but it was certainly in a condition that was acceptable for habitation. He said they were closing on October 30 and I could move in immediately after they closed. We just needed the baby to stay in the oven until November 1.

In late October Gilda came home and told me that she went to her prenatal appointment and the doctor said the baby was in distress. The doctor went on to tell Gilda that she needed to return to the hospital the next day and they were going to remove the baby via C-Section. The next day we returned to the hospital and I watched as the doctor cut my wife's stomach open and removed my daughter. The baby wasn't crying like I would normally see on TV. The nurse brought her to a table with a lamp over it and seconds later, I heard her scream. Seeing that Gilda was still slightly sedated I named her Toni.

When we left the hospital several days later Gilda decided to go to her mother's house since she felt unwelcome at the apartment we shared with Russell. November 1, 1998 we moved into our new apartment on Draper Street in Dorchester. I was comforted to know that there was a Boston Police Homicide Detective living across the street from us.

The house had two bedrooms and it was ours. In East Boston the community looked out for each other. On Draper Street they were shooting at each other. The Cape Verdeans shot at each other and anyone that happened to be in the area when they decided to pull their guns. Gilda went back to work at Mount Auburn Hospital during the morning shift. During the day I watched Toni while Francis was in school.

One morning I woke up to find that my car had been stolen. We got another car with a better security system in it. One night while at home with Gilda and the kids, I heard gun shots being fired outside, and they seemed really close. I grabbed a gun and went to the front door. When I got there I saw the detective from across the street running down the street with gun in hand. I went back in to the house and called 911 and told them what happened. I wanted to run and help him, but had I ran out of my house with a gun in hand, I would have appeared to be just another black man with a gun. Nothing good could come of that even though I had good intentions. I went to my car the next morning and discovered that my car had three bullet holes in it from the shooting the night before. I decided not to get the holes fixed at that moment. I saw the detective a few days later and explained to him that I was a special police officer. I went on to explain that I saw him running down the street a few days before. I told him if it happened again, I would be happy to assist him if he wanted. He assured me that I should NOT assist. He confirmed what I already knew. If other officers arrived on the scene and saw me there with a gun, nothing good could come of it. We agreed that I would simply be a good witness.

I worked the 4pm - 12am shift while Gilda worked the morning shift. A few months later, while Francis was walking home from school she had to walk around a crime scene where someone had been killed and they were actively investigating the shooting. I decided then that we had to get out of that house. It was too dangerous to raise a family with two small daughters.

That year on four separate occasions, my car was shot. There were so many shooting incidents on Draper Street I thought we had moved to a war zone. In September 1999, Shelton's sister informed me that she was doubling my rent. I was furious. Living in the house meant my family had to risk their lives and she had the audacity to not just raise my rent, but to double it. I spoke with Shelton and he seemed to have been just as shocked as I was. If they wanted me to move, all they had to do was ask. Coincidentally, at that same time Gilda's parents, who owned a two family house, said their tenants on the first floor were moving out. Gilda asked if we could have the apartment and they agreed. Therefore, on November 1, 1999, we moved in to their first floor apartment.

It was a relief living in a secure and stable environment. Toni was proving to clearly be a daddy's girl. I wish I had the words to explain why or how, but she and I just seemed to click. With that said, all children misbehave and when she did, she was punished. When I decided that Toni needed a spanking, she and I would go into my room and talk for hours about what happened, why it happened, what she did, what could have happened, what she should have done and why this amounted to a spanking. Gilda hated when I spanked Toni. Not because she was against the idea of spanking, but just that it took so long.

I never ever struck my kids in anger. If they didn't understand the lesson, then spanking them was simply a waste of time, and they would most likely repeat the same actions again. I figured if I corrected the thought process, the problem would be solved long term. Gilda wanted me to just spank her and get it over with. I tried for years to explain that was not my idea of how to discipline children. Gilda wasn't a spanker, she preferred to yell and leave the spanking to me.

Toni and Francis were each different in their academic aptitudes. However, Toni and I developed an awesome communication rapport.

95

When Toni was 10, I asked her if she was pro-life or pro-choice. After explaining the difference, we would debate her response. No matter what she said I always presented the other side of the argument. I did this with all the kids that regularly visited my house. It was important that they be aware of all the angles presented and be able to explain themselves, no matter what they thought.

I felt that communication was the key to any relationship whether it was a business relationship, romantic relationship, a friendship or a family relationship. The ability to openly and honestly communicate one's thoughts in a manner that was both clear and respectful was important. This character trait remains with me to this day.

Toni at the age of 4 started to take dance lessons in Tap, Jazz, Ballet, and Lyrical. Francis wasn't interested, so we didn't force her. Toni continued these dance lessons until she was 15 years old. I have always had a philosophy on the kids and their grades. My philosophy is that mom and dad go to work. At the end of the week we bring home a paycheck. We turn that check in to cash and with that cash we pay bills, go on vacation and buy other things. On the other hand kids go to work too, it's called school. They too get a paycheck; it's called a report card. Now before they get their first report card, we extend them credit and buy the things they want. But when they get their paychecks (report card), they have to pay for all the things they have gotten to that date. I feel like our kids need to know that they are expected to be successful.

They also need to know that success doesn't come easily. It comes through hard work and determination. If they were willing to put in the hard work, I would be prepared to reward them. If they were not willing to put in the hard work, I would do whatever I could to make their lives miserable. This was not done out of boredom; this was because of my experiences of how life is.

In life when you work hard, generally good things come, but when you don't life is uncomfortable. By the time Toni reached 16 years old I became frustrated with her poor grades. Therefore, I developed a different philosophy. My new philosophy is that ballet is for people who have expendable income. Getting the grades Toni was getting I didn't imagine she would have any expendable income because she would most likely not get a good job forcing her to live in low income housing developments. I felt she needed to learn to fight. So I removed her from dance class and enrolled her in Boxing, Muy Thai and Krav Maga. We also went to the range regularly so she could learn to responsibly handle a firearm. Interestingly enough, she liked it more than I thought she would. She isn't an MMA fighter or anything, but I am teaching her to think tactically and how to protect herself as a young woman.

We debate regularly and this has given her the confidence to be able to express herself to me and in her daily interactions with others. Because of the level of communication we both enjoy, she knew that when I disciplined her, it is because I love her and I know she has the potential to achieve more.

10

Trust...years to build, seconds to break

I continued to work as a Special Police Officer at New World Security, where I found myself arresting people for doing things members of my family did all my life. Some of the areas I patrolled were in the same area I lived as a child. Other places we patrolled were low-income housing developments. Some people in these developments paid less than $100 per month in rent, while others paid over $1,000 to live in the same building. Although I met some good people working in Boston, there were also people who were just trying to take advantage of people in the community by committing robberies, breaking and entering, selling drugs and other crimes of violence against members of the community.

The job was a blast and very fulfilling. The fulfillment I got from arresting some of these people was unexplainable. I suggested to Aaron that he come work with me, but he wasn't interested. He was happy working with copy machines. He seemed to be pretty good at it too. One day I was told that I was going to be permanently assigned to work with Sgt. Maria Wilburn. Sgt. Wilburn was a large woman compared to me. She was 5'11" tall, and about 260 pounds. I on the other hand was 5'6" tall weighing in at 150 pounds.

I was happy with my new assignment. I didn't know Sgt. Wilburn, but it turned out that she had a lot of experience and seemed to know her way around the streets. After a couple of months of working with Sgt. Wilburn I figured out that she was selling marijuana while on duty. She would get a phone call on her cell phone and would suddenly need to go home. Immediately after leaving her house, we would go and meet someone who was not working at our company, nor did they appear to have anything to do with the developments we were contracted to patrol. When I thought I realized what she was doing I simply asked her,

"Sergeant?"

"What's up?" She responded.

Nervously I said, "If I didn't know any better, I'd think you were selling something."

"What makes you say that?" She said while stopping the car on a side street for no apparent reason and then stared me down.

I swallowed and then said, "First, you get a call and you talk on your phone for about 10-15 seconds. Then we stop what we're doing and go to your house where you go in and seem to come right back out. We then drive directly to a location we have no reason to be, where you go just inside of the door of someone's house and come back out to the car."

The look on her face said to me that she didn't realize I was paying attention. I continued,

"Usually when you're on the phone talking to family or a friend, you stay on the phone for a few minutes at least. But I know when you hang up after talking for just a few seconds, the odds are that we are on our way to your house."

She looked at me for a few minutes and then said, "And what do you think I'm selling".

I said, "I have no idea, but seeing that you don't keep it in the car very long, it's obviously against policy. The only thing I can guess is that it's something illegal."

She said, "ok, we're cool I think I can trust you. I sell a little weed from time to time. When I'm talking on the phone for a short period of time, it's a customer and I have to go to my house to pick up what they want and bring it directly to them". She then said, "Keep your mouth shut because snitches get stitches".

It was her way of threatening my life if I reported it. I was in shock and didn't know what to say. I couldn't believe this was happening. I had gone out of my way during my life to that point not to be involved with drugs. Now, here I was in essence dealing drugs myself. She seemed to be relieved that she didn't have to continue to hide what she was doing. She started to drive again and we went on to the next topic of conversation. I felt like my heart was going to jump out of my chest.

To say I was between a rock and a hard place was putting it lightly. During this period, I was friendly with Lieutenant Wolfe, so I decided I would tell him what took place and asked his advice, off the record.

He said, "There have been rumors of Sgt. Wilburn doing that for years." I was in shock, "Well why doesn't someone do something about it" I asked?

He suggested I officially report it and let the cards fall where they may. I said, "Easy for you to say, you aren't the one who has to ride with her". I had to plan my moves perfectly or literally risk my life. He promised to keep quiet for a couple days until I figured out what to do.

The next day after reporting for duty, Sgt. Wilburn was silent. She said nothing to me, no greeting, no instructions, no briefing, nothing. We got in the car and she started to drive. About 15 minutes later, she then pulled the car over on Talbot Ave and instructed me to get out of the car. There was no reason for us to be at this part of Talbot Ave. I suddenly got a bad feeling as she got out of the driver's side door, walked down the street and motioned for me to follow her. I followed her and when we were about 50 yards from the car she stopped, turned to me and said,

"So you told Lt. Wolfe I was selling weed?"

My jaw hit the floor. I didn't know what to say. We were on a sidewalk on a public street that was busy with rush hour traffic. All I could remember at that moment was her saying,

"Keep your mouth shut cause snitches get stitches".

I didn't think she was going to shoot me right there. I thought for a second we were going to fight, so I got ready. I wouldn't normally be ready to fight a woman but seeing that she was built like a man, I had no choice. She went on to tell me that she had friends much higher than the Lieutenant, and if I opened my mouth again, I'd never make it home. She turned, walked to the car, got in and waited for me to get in. We didn't speak about it again and she continued to sell weed on duty. This Sergeant was my partner and as such, primary back-up.

I had recently been married and was about to either lose my life or my ability to support my family. All she had to do was wait for a call to go bad and not back me up. I learned a lesson I would take with me for the rest of my law enforcement career. I learned to *"Never get myself into anything I can't get myself out of."*

As I sat in the car I contemplated my options. Obviously I could not trust my command staff. As far as I was concerned I was on my own. I considered simply leaving the job, but I needed to support my family, and we had no savings. Therefore quitting was not an option. I decided to go the legal route. The problem is that for my claim to stand up in a court I would need evidence. I thought an allegation like this would be unbelievable without evidence, because the only time she had the drugs on her was when she was going to drop them off. I decided to go to the Boston Police Department in area C-11 and spoke to Sergeant Daley from the drug unit. I told Sgt. Daley everything I knew and he asked me if I'd be willing to work with him and his guys to resolve the issue. I said,

"Of course I would".

He called New World Security and spoke with Benjamin "Ben" White on speaker. Ben White was in charge of the day-to-day operations of New World Security. Sgt. Daley told Ben that he wanted me to work with his guys to resolve the situation. Ben White already appeared to be aware of the situation and told Sgt. Daley that not only was I not permitted to work with the Boston Police on this, but if he discovered I was working with them, I'd be fired. Sgt. Daley asked me what I wanted to do. He went on to say that if they found drugs in my patrol vehicle and I'm not working with his guys being part of the solution, he would have to make the assumption that I was part of the problem. I told him I needed some time to think. The next day, Sgt. Wilburn handed in her resignation. I decided to let things ride until she left. Two weeks later Sgt. Wilburn was gone. I heard she had gotten a job working for the MBTA, driving a bus.

11

Francis

From the moment Jessica and I split up, I spent every possible weekend with my daughter. I made sure I paid child support and even sent additional money as needed when I was able. On some weekends when I had to work, Gilda would agree to watch Francis. After work on Sundays, I'd pick Francis up from Gilda's house and bring her home. The stories Francis told us about some things that happened at her mother's house made it clear that she needed these weekend breaks with me. At one point Francis who was 5 years old showed Gilda's mother how to roll a blunt using seasonings and tissue.

When I picked Francis up for my weekend visits, she was usually dirty, with clothes that seemed to be too small, torn or in some way made her appear unkempt. I asked Jessica about her appearance and she would simply reply, "If you don't like what Francis is wearing, then buy her new clothes." As a result Gilda or I would often go and buy Francis new clothes to wear. When we did, we threw her old clothes in the trash. We started to realize that when we sent Francis home in the new clothes we purchased, she always returned to me in the most inappropriate clothes forcing me to buy her new clothes. Then at some point we got frustrated and instead of discarding the old clothes Francis came to us in, we kept them and put them back on her when it was time to take her home. I felt horrible doing it, but I felt like I was being taken advantage of.

Francis's first day of school at Head Start was difficult. Jessica and I both went with her. When we walked through the entrance, and explained to Francis that she had to go to school, she started to cry. Jessica attempted to calm her down but she was failing miserably. I dropped down to one knee, pulled Francis to me and gave her a big hug and asked her to stop crying so I could talk to her. When she calmed herself down I explained,

"Baby, daddy loves you but you simply must go to school we don't have a choice". She started to cry again saying she didn't want to go. So I said, "I know you don't want to go but what you need to understand is that you have 12 years of school and then you'll have three choices, college, the military or your own place, because I raise kids, I don't raise adults. Now, if you decide to go to college you'll have four more years of school." She got this look of complete confusion on her face. I then asked, "Do you understand baby girl?" She was only 5 years old at the time, and Jessica looked at me with this look of pure horror.

Francis then said, "Daddy, what's College?"

I said, "Don't worry about it baby I'll explain it later, for now just know you've got to figure this school thing out. So turn around and go say hi to your teacher" and she did.

One day when my daughter was in the kindergarten, I went to get her for my weekly visit, but Jessica told me that she was with her grandfather, Ernest, for the weekend. I said,

"Okay, I'll just see her next weekend."

I gave her the child support and left. Around that time, Jessica had married a guy named Kuma and I heard a rumor that week that Jessica's house was raided by the Boston Police Department. I had never known Jessica to be involved with any drugs in any way, so I did not believe it.

The next weekend, I went to get Francis, and was told by Jessica that Francis was with Ernest's ex-wife for the weekend. I was angry, and I told her that I didn't care who wanted to spend time with her the following weekend, I hadn't seen Francis in three weeks and the next weekend she was going to be spending it with me. Once again, I gave Jessica the child support and left. The following weekend I went to get

Francis and again I was told she was with someone else. Needless to say I was furious. I said angrily, "Absolutely not. This weekend is my weekend. Where is she?" Jessica wouldn't tell me. I insisted and she still refused to tell me where Francis was. We had an argument, after which I left furious.

During that following week, while I was at work, I saw my daughter's maternal uncle. I stopped and asked him if he knew where Francis was. He said, "Yeah, Francis has been with us for three weeks. We can't find Jessica." I instructed him to get into my patrol vehicle and take me to Francis. When I saw Francis, she looked like she hadn't changed clothes in weeks. The truth is she hadn't.

I discovered that Francis had been staying with her maternal grandmother, Deborah, for the last three weeks. Deborah was born with some birth defects. She had no forearms. Her hands were where her elbows were supposed to be and she only had three or four fingers on each hand. In this condition Deborah still had eight children. She was on welfare and never worked. She drank a lot and in later years Jessica would tell me Deborah was also addicted to crack cocaine.

Deborah and I had a good relationship while Jessica and I were dating. She had even allowed me to sleep at her house from time to time, just not in the bed with Jessica. After Jessica and I broke up, I never saw her, so when I got to her house I had no idea what to expect. I walked in with Freddy and Francis and greeted Deborah with a hug and kiss on the cheek as I had always done. I explained to Deborah why I was there and that I intended to leave with Francis. Deborah told me that three weeks prior; Jessica dropped Francis off for what was supposed to be ten minutes. She left no change of clothes, no money for food, no contact number and three weeks later they still couldn't find Jessica.

At my request, Deborah wrote and signed a statement indicating what she told me. I left some money with her in an attempt to thank her for taking care of Francis for the last three weeks, and took my daughter. On the following Monday, I took Francis to school and went to a Boston Police Officer friend and asked if he could confirm whether Jessica's house was raided. He not only confirmed it, but gave me the police report. I was horrified to learn that cocaine was not only found in the house, it was literally found in Francis's bedroom.

I took the statement from Deborah and the police report to court, filed for and received temporary emergency custody of Francis. As instructed by the court, I mailed Jessica all court paperwork including the custody motion. In anticipation of Jessica responding to the motion and my having to defend my decision in court, I started to gather my evidence. I already had the police report and letter from Deborah. I went to Francis's school and obtained her school records. I was shocked to learn that Francis missed 62% of school that year.

How Francis was not required to repeat kindergarten remains a mystery to me. 18 months later, Jessica still hadn't responded to my motion. When Jessica did respond we had to go back to court so that permanent custody could be decided. By then Francis's life changed dramatically for the better. She went from missing 62% of school and barely making it out of K-1, to not only having good attendance, but being an honor roll student.

Francis went from living in a house where cocaine was actively being sold, to living in a stable home with structure, consistency, love and support. It was no surprise that after hearing all the evidence, the Judge decided that Francis should remain with me. I was ecstatic. The judge asked me if I wanted to request child support from Jessica, and I told the Judge I didn't want child support. I declined child support for two reasons. First, I wasn't rich by any stretch of the imagination, but I didn't need her money to take care of my daughter. Secondly, I figured having your child taken away from you must be hard and I was not going to make it any harder on Jessica. I could not imagine what it must have felt like being a mother and having a child you gave life to taken away from you. Even though I was trying to sympathize with her, I didn't care enough to risk her damaging my daughter any more than she may have already done. I was determined to have Francis live a better life than the one I had, and I was willing to put in all required work to achieve my goal. I felt confident that I now had the opportunity to prove that she could have a better life.

Jessica picked Francis up for visits on an inconsistent basis. Although she was permitted to take Francis every weekend, she was supposed to bring her back by 6pm on Sunday. This never happened before she always brought Francis home late. When I called Jessica, she wouldn't answer my calls. Francis almost never returned home before 10 pm. Most weeks, Francis came home after midnight and frequently after 2 am Monday knowing Francis had school in the morning. Then in addition to bringing Francis home late, Jessica would call my house and scream at Gilda about decisions I made in regards to Francis.

After several years of consistently fighting with Jessica about these issues, I decided that if Jessica insisted on disrupting my household, she needed to pay for the privilege. Therefore I went to court and asked for child support. I didn't need the money, but I was angry. With that being said, there was no reason Jessica should not contribute to taking care of her daughter. Many other non-custodial parents did it all the time all over the country. When we went to court, the judge ordered Jessica to pay $20 per week. Jessica had relocated to New York and the judge stated the cost of living in New York was higher than in Boston so she didn't think it was appropriate to have Jessica pay what the guidelines said she should pay. Jessica literally laughed when the judge said $20 a week. I was furious. Years later her child support payments would be in the arrears in excess of $5,000.00.

In the meantime, Francis excelled in school. When she was in the 5th grade, she and Aunt Nicole asked if I would allow Francis to go to a private, more challenging school. Francis's teacher told us that Francis would be in school reading an unrelated book or in some cases sleeping and when the teacher handed out a test Francis would put her book down, take the test, finish it faster than any other student and score

100%. Gilda and I ended up agreeing to allow Francis the opportunity to attend an independent school.

After an exhaustive search, we decided that she would attend the Windsor School. When I learned that the cost was $23,000.00 a year, I was overwhelmed. I thought there was no way we could afford this. However, having made the decision to pursue this path, we ended up getting some financial aid, but still had to pay $11,000.00 plus books and fees. I figured if I wanted her to not replicate my life, this was what needed to happen. I asked Jessica if she was willing to assist me with paying Francis's tuition. Jessica said she wasn't contributing to independent schools, unless I could pay for it out of her $20 a week child support money. Therefore, Gilda and I made some sacrifices and in the 6th grade, Francis started to attend The Windsor School.

The Windsor School was an all-girls independent school in the Fenway section of Boston. We had to drive Francis to school daily. The young girls that attended this school appeared to be nothing less than exceptional. Some of these girls were dropped off by limousines. When the chauffeur opened the door for these girls, they got out, not wearing backpacks, but carrying brief cases. I almost took Francis home the first time I saw a 6th grader get out of a limo carrying a briefcase. I had faith in Francis's ability to succeed. I remember saying to myself, "If these are the issues my daughter had to face, I can live with that".

Unfortunately, I didn't realize the effect this affluent environment would have on Francis. We soon realized that the Windsor did not seem to be a good fit for her. It did not provide the kind of support she needed. So, we started looking for a different school for her to attend in the 7th grade. We applied to many schools, however one school seemed to be better suited to her needs than the others, but there was a catch. The Fay School was $32,000.00 a year, but the major issue was it was a boarding school. Gilda was completely against Francis living at school at such a young age. Francis would be about 12 years old and living at school on her own. Jessica had no opinion. The only thing Jessica said was that she was not contributing. Aunt Nicole, who was an educator at Phillips Academy, Andover, wanted Francis to go to the Fay School.

In the end, I sat down with Francis and explained the issues. I told her that my fear was that her not being at home would most likely mean that she would not be as close to the family. I explained that there would be times when it would be hard for us to assist her when she needed it, because we simply wouldn't know what was going on with her on a daily basis. It meant that Francis would have to learn to advocate for herself. With that said, The Fay School had an excellent reputation and I truly thought it would give Francis the best option for success.

During this time, Gilda and Francis were not getting along and, I may not have done the best job of managing their issues. I decided to allow Francis to go. Before she left, I reminded Francis that I thought I was choosing between her ability to get into a good college and have a better life, or she and I being close. I decided it was better for her to have a bright future than it was for the two of us to have a great relationship, yet I still hoped we would. I figured in time we could always work on our relationship. In the 7th and 8th grade she went to the Fay School, costing us $32,000.00 and $36,000.00 respectively.

All four years of high school were at Phillips Academy Andover, with a price tag of $50,000.00 per year. Thank GOD she was able to get a scholarship to attend Phillips Academy. After graduating Phillips Academy, she was accepted into Dartmouth College in New Hampshire, which further drew a cost of $50,000.00 per year. She graduated with her Bachelor's degree in Romance languages and Sociology in 2012. At this point, due to a number of misunderstandings she and I no longer speak because she believes I don't love her. Obviously she couldn't be more wrong. Most parents try to make choices for their children so that they can have a better life than they did, however these intentions are sometimes misunderstood by young teens as they go through inevitable mood swings.

12

No Pain, No Gain

I quit New World Security after working there for 5 years and was hired by Naratoone Security. There wasn't any major difference between New World and Naratoone Security. Mass Housing/HUD contracted both security companies to provide police services to different housing developments throughout the city of Boston. Though both were very similar, the only real difference was that New World Security was contracted to patrol Mass Housing Developments. This meant that the developments we patrolled were owned by MassHousing, a state agency.

Naratoone Security patrolled housing developments that were owned by the Department of Housing and Urban Development, (HUD) a federal agency. On the administrative side, one other major difference was that Naratoone Security paid 25% more hourly than New World Security. In essence I was paid almost double by Naratoone Security to do the exact same job in the same areas of Boston. After a couple of years at Naratoone Security, I was promoted to Sergeant. As a special officer we had very few benefits. I had two weeks annual vacation, with no health insurance, no retirement, no 401(k) and no stability. In addition, every year we ran the risk of our company not getting the security contract and having to look for work elsewhere. Although we had few benefits, we were well paid.

A number of the officers at Naratoone had motorcycles. I wanted a motorcycle for a long time. Seeing that most of my coworkers were riding in on them, they became a frequent topic of discussion between Gilda and me. On father's day one year, my wife got me motorcycle lessons. After taking this course I was able to get a motorcycle endorsement on my drivers' license. Gilda figured that after taking the class, I probably would have gotten the motorcycle bug out of my system. Boy was she wrong. A couple of years later, I purchased a bike of my own. She had agreed to me purchasing a bike under the condition that I always rode with a high quality motorcycle jacket, boot and gloves regardless of the weather. It was uncomfortable, but I made it a point to comply with our agreement whenever I rode. My first bike was a used Honda CBR 600cc. It was a nice bike, but wasn't very fast. I liked to ride with groups of riders. It didn't matter where we rode, and often we had no destination, we just rode.

A few months after having my bike, I had it parked in the front of my house overnight and when I came out the next morning, it was gone. I was very upset to lose that bike, but Gilda agreed with my decision to purchase a new motorcycle. After some searching, I bought a Ducati 900 Sport Touring bike. It was yellow with a half faring. I had never quite seen a bike like this. It wasn't a sport bike, but I liked it and kept it for two years. A number of guys I rode with had the Yamaha R1 and I liked that bike a lot. It was sexy, and fast. It was no surprise that in 2003, I traded in my Ducati for a new 2003 Yamaha R1. I started paying for it January of 2003 and on April 1, 2003 I rode it home. It was everything I hoped it would have been. Of course, Gilda encouraged me to get matching boots, jacket and gloves.

On April 15, 2003, exactly two weeks after I drove the bike home, I was riding in Boston with some friends. We were hanging out at Washington Park in Roxbury watching guys go up and down the street doing tricks on their bikes. At some point three guys rode up to Tony, one of the guys I was riding with, and after exchanging greetings' Tony introduced him to us. His name was Jeffrey. Jeffrey's bike was Pepsi blue and it had the word "PEPSI' all over it. Tony later explained that Jeffrey was a semi-professional motorcycle racer, and Pepsi bought his bike for him. This obviously explained the paint job. A short while after, Jeffrey began riding up and down the street on one wheel. I was always too afraid to try wheeling. First, if Gilda found out, my riding days would be over, and second I didn't want to risk falling and messing up my bike. After a while, Jeffrey and his boys left and my group of friends continued to ride.

At some point I decided to go home. I was near the Mass. Ave entrance to 93N, so I decided to take the expressway home. As soon as I entered the expressway, I saw Jeffrey and his boys. I decided to catch up to them and ride with them as far as I could on my way home. Jeffrey was the first bike, there was a bike between us and I was the third bike, with two bikes behind me. The Ted Williams Tunnel had just opened, and this was my first time going through it in this direction. As we entered the tunnel, Jeffrey sped off. As he entered the tunnel the road declined and turned to the right, but Jeffrey seemed to go straight, hitting the wall. The collision caused Jeffrey to separate from his bike, both of them taking up the two left lanes, and there was a car in the right lane. The bike in front of me seemed to try to go left between Jeffrey, who was now sliding on his back, and his bike. Unfortunately he struck Jeffrey's lower body and was thrown off of his bike. I attempted to go right around Jeffrey, but the impact from the other bike hitting him caused him to spin and slide directly in front of me. Since I was already in a turn, I was unable to correct, and go around him. Therefore I had no choice then to go over Jeffrey's upper body, and was thrown from my bike. It seemed like I was in flight for quite some time and then I rotated mid-air and landed on my back. Luckily, I was wearing all of the safety equipment Gilda insisted that I wear. As I got to my feet, all of the traffic on 93 north had come to a stop, and I saw Jeffrey seemingly lifeless body on the ground of the expressway. I rushed over to him in an attempt to try to provide some type of aid to him, but a car stopped and a woman in a hospital scrubs got out of her car. She said she was a nurse and was doing CPR on him. A minute to two later she stopped and said he was dead and there was nothing she could do. Because we were in the tunnel, there was no cellular reception, so as cars passed by us we motion and yelled out for the drivers to call 911 and get us some help. It seemed like forever, but the police arrived with an ambulance and soon after I was taken to the hospital.

While I was in the back of the ambulance, as soon as I got out of the tunnel, I called my wife and told her what had happened and she said she was on her way to the hospital. I also called Tony to give him the tragic news and the only thing I heard on the other end was Tony bursting into tears. Once at the hospital, the doctors told me that I broke my wrist in the accident, and had to put a cast on my arm. Since we had no sick time at Naratoone, I continued to work as a police officer, with a broken arm.

A few days later I was told that the police were considering charging me with vehicular homicide. The police report stated while traveling on 93 north, my bike struck Jeffrey' bike, causing him to go in to the wall. This couldn't be further from the truth. I contacted an attorney who instructed me not to talk to anyone including the police about this incident. Later that week, a coworker told me that Jeffrey's brother had recently gotten out of jail after killing someone. He said this brother was a member of the "Humboldt Street Gang" and that they wanted revenge for his brother's death. I had been carrying a gun every day for years before that. However I was told to be on guard and to watch my back. "From whom" I thought. I didn't even know what this guy looked like. Who was I watching out for?

A couple of weeks later Tony called me and told me that Jeffrey' brother wanted to talk to me. I told him I was instructed by my attorney not to talk about the accident. I also told Tony I heard his brother was coming after me and I didn't want to antagonize the situation. Tony assured me that there was no hostile intent coming from this brother. He said they just want to know what happened. Again I refused on my attorney's instructions. He said ok, we exchanged pleasantries and we hung up.

The next day, Tony called me again. He said Jeffrey's family wanted to speak to me and that they weren't trying to cause any issues, but just wanted some information on the accident. The accident was still under investigation and as such, the police were not releasing any information. He pleaded with me to talk to him and against my lawyer's advice, so I called his brother.

William was pleasant, but I could tell by the way he spoke, that he was from the streets. Will told me he heard that Tony had said that he was coming after me. He said he was recently released from prison after serving 18 years for a murder he committed in Boston, and if anyone in his family was going to be coming after me it would be him. He was in Florida with no intentions of coming to Boston. He went on to say that Jeffrey loved motorcycles and they always knew if Jeffrey died early, it would have something to do with motorcycles. He said they had some details of the accident and just wanted specifics from someone who was there. I told him everything I knew. He said they just needed to know if Jeffrey was in pain before he died.

The truth is I had no idea, but I told him I didn't think he felt anything at all. At the conclusion of the police investigation, I wasn't charged with a crime. Gilda said the next time I come home with a motorcycle, I should make sure I also have divorce papers with me. That was the end of my riding days.

13

Embracing our differences

Around this time Gilda had a cousin Jacques who came to Boston from Haiti under the premise of being on vacation. His true intention was to relocate to the United States. Jacques was 18 years old and being from Haiti spoke only Creole. After moving in to my in-laws house, he started high school at Somerville High School in the 9th grade. When I met Jacques I felt something about him wasn't right. I didn't know what it was but I wasn't comfortable with him being around. Because I didn't know why I felt this way, I kept my feelings to myself figuring I just needed to get to know him.

A few months after school started, my mother in-law Violetta, found a gay porn magazine in Jacques room. Being 60 or so years old, she was understandably uncomfortable with the images she saw. When Jacques returned home that day, she asked him about the magazines and Jacques told her he found the magazines and felt uncomfortable putting them in the trash, so he put them under his mattress. Not knowing much about homosexuality, my mother in-law believed him. Being gay in the Haitian community was unacceptable. My mother in-law tore the magazines into small pieces and put them into the trash. When Violetta told Gil about the incident, Gil asked me to talk to him and see if he was gay. By this time Jacques had begun to speak some broken English. I enlisted the language assistance of my brother in-law Ronny who was born in Haiti and still had a good command of the language. Ronny hesitated initially saying he was very uncomfortable, but in the end, he agreed to translate only. Through Ronny, I asked Jacques if he was gay, he said he wasn't. I told him if he was we would accept him, but there were things that were and were not appropriate. I was lying. I was disgusted with having this conversation with him and hoped there was a reasonable explanation he could give us as to why he had the magazines. If he was gay, I imagined it meant he probably victimized some defenseless child or children in Haiti before coming to the United States. Even worse, I'd have to keep him out of my house or risk having to kill him for victimizing my children. If he laid an inappropriate hand on my kids, I'd do things to him that would definitely land me in jail and him in a coffin.

Jacques swore he wasn't "Macesee", which was the Haitian slur for gay. I explained to him that there was no way a straight man would bring home magazines like the ones Violetta found in his room. He insisted he wasn't gay. When I felt my interrogation was no longer progressing in a positive direction, I ended by saying he could always talk to me and that I wouldn't judge him. Again I was lying. I hoped he wasn't gay and if he was, I hoped he never brought it to my attention. I simply didn't want to know. For the next year or so, Jacques got better with his English and we were able to communicate without the assistance of translators. Attending Somerville High School forced him to learn English.

One day, Gil called me and told me Jacques was being suspended from school for inappropriately touching a boy in his class. Again she asked if I could talk to him. Although I had become more comfortable with him I didn't think I was comfortable enough to deal with this issue in a fair way. She said no one else would talk to him, so I said I would. I called Ronny and insisted he be with me. This time I didn't need his language skills but I wanted him there with me anyway. I told Gil to have Jacques wait for me in his room and I would talk to him when I got home. Ronny and I met in my house, which was downstairs from my in-laws house. I told Ronny I had a plan. My plan was to explain to Jacques that seeing that he was an adult, if he ever inappropriately touched juveniles, he could go to jail. I went on to tell

Ronny that at some point it's going to look like I snapped and I was going to attack Jacques. I wasn't going to punch or hit him, but was going to jostle him, scare him and put him in hand cuffs because that's what was going to happen to him if he touched another juvenile. Ronny chuckled and said okay. He wasn't sure what I was going do, but he agreed to play along.

We went up to Jacques room and we started to talk to him. Again I asked him if he was gay and again he said he wasn't. He said he was just joking with the kid in school. I told him even Stevie Wonder could see he was gay. I explained to him what Frank had done to me and that he was family and although I didn't like homosexuals, he (Jacques), was family and I accepted and supported him. I told him how I thought homosexuals tested out their perversions on children and asked if he had ever abused a child. He said he hadn't and that he wasn't gay.

At that point I felt like the situation was not a big deal, so I lunged at him grabbing him by the collar of his shirt and lifted him from the bed he was sitting on and then throwing him back on to it. All the while I was yelling at him "Is this how you want to be treated by either the police or some guy in jail?" Ronny looked at me in pure shock. It was almost like his fear of what was going on stopped him from moving. I ripped Jacques from the bed again and pinned him face first to the wall yelling at him again. Jacques started to whimper and talk in Creole. I continued yelling at him, "Is this how you want to be treated?" At this point I could see that he was crying and tears were running down his face. I ripped him from the wall and threw him to the bed again hard, grabbed one of his hands, put it behind his back and put a handcuff on it. I told him to give me his other hand and he refused, maybe he was so scared that he probably didn't understand what I was asking him to do. I put his wrist in a wrist-lock, a technique I used at work a lot when arresting people and the pain he started to feel helped him to understand what I was asking of him. He gave me his other hand and I put the other handcuff on him and sat him up on the bed. I asked Jacques if he enjoyed how I had just treated him and with tears running down his face, he said "no". I explained to him that if he touched another kid; he'd likely feel that treatment again but next time it wouldn't be by a family member. It would be by someone who didn't care about him or what he felt.

Ronny still hadn't moved an inch and judging by the look on his face he probably hoped he wouldn't get the same treatment. I took the handcuffs off of Jacques and told him that we all knew he was gay and that as soon as he admitted it, we as a family would do what we could to guide him as best we could, but if he touched any kid he'd probably land in jail and if he touched my kids, he'd land in a grave. Ronny continued to sit still, silent and in awe of the situation. Shortly after I told Ronny to get up because that we were leaving. Ronny did as instructed and we left. About a week later Jacques approached me while I was in my kitchen. He looked at me with this look of shame, with his head bowed looking at the floor and said, "I'm gay". I told him we knew he was and it was okay.

14

Life's Getting Better

It's pretty ironic that a young inner city kid who was surrounded by drugs and crime would grow up to have a professional career in law enforcement but that is what happened. After being a special officer for ten years, I decided that I needed more of a future for my family in order to give them a better life than what I had growing up. I believe that as a father and husband, your family relies on your ability to provide them with a safe home and environment and this largely depends on your ability to afford it. So, the search for a better opportunity began.

Although I worked for a security company, my employer was subcontracted through MassHousing. The owners of the security company answered to Thaddeus Miles, the Director of Public Safety for MassHousing. At one point Thaddeus offered to sponsor anyone who wanted to attend the full-time police Academy. Sponsorship simply meant he'd provide his signature. Whoever accepted his offer would still have to pay the $5,000 to the academy plus get all the required equipment. In addition, I would need to save enough money to pay household bills for six months. Working while training was prohibited. This added to the fact that I did not have a job secured if or when I graduated the academy. At the time he offered sponsorship, I didn't take him up on it because I simply was not financially or physically prepared. After much thought I told my wife I needed to find a way to get into the academy. I knew she'd support me as she always did. Having the support of a loving spouse gives you immeasurable rewards. So after hearing her positive feedback, I spoke to Thaddeus and being a man of his word he agreed to sponsor me in the academy. I saved up as much money as I could and borrowed the rest from my brother-in-law.

Along with coming up with the money, I now had to focus on getting my body in shape for training. It would have been a waste of time and money for me to pay for the academy but fail the training because I was out of shape. I was 5'6" tall and 220 pounds and had never been in shape a day of my life. So being the strategic man that I am, every other day I ran two miles in order to get in shape. I knew I couldn't afford to fail. When I received the start date for the academy I put in my two-week notice at my job and it felt great! I started the Reading Regional Police Academy in January 2003.

The first few days at the academy were pretty routine that was focused primarily on administrative things and making sure we had all the required equipment. On Wednesday of that week we did our physical training assessment, which meant a mile and a half run around a track. I'd been practicing this run for months and was ready for it. I completed the run in the middle of my class. In light of me having never been in shape before and also most of my class being at least 10 years younger than I was and fresh out of the military, I was happy with my progress. The following day, we had our first class run.

During the run I noticed that I had some pain in my right foot. I made the assumption it was just my body working out the kinks. On Friday we ran again and my foot continued to hurt but I sucked it up and ran through it. Unfortunately for me, the pain got worse the more I ran. On that Friday I went to the emergency room and discovered I had a stress fracture in my right foot. The hospital gave me a walking cast and sent me on my way. I presented the documentation to the police academy on Monday and told them what the hospital had diagnosed, as academy rules required. The director of the academy, Rhoda Pires, along with the senior staff instructor Richard Lebel informed me that as a result of my injury I could no longer continue my training and had to drop out of the academy. To say this was a major disappointment is an understatement. I told them I needed to stay. I had no place to go and no job to return to. I told them I would run on the broken foot and I would sign any waiver they needed me to in order to release the academy from liability. They stood their ground and said no. I had no option, I had to leave. I was devastated. I collected my things, went back to my car.

A lot of thoughts were racing through my head like how was I now going to support my family, what was next for me? As I sat in my car in the parking lot of the academy, I let the tears run down my face as I figured out what my next move was. What was I supposed to do? How can I go home and tell my wife I was kicked out of the academy? How was I going to take care of my wife and kids and give them the life they deserved? It was a gamble for me to quit work to go to the academy, and I bet on the wrong horse.

Quitting a job is always a risk and the reality is that sometimes it pays off and sometimes it doesn't. I decided to go back to work and beg for my old job back. It was a long shot, and required humility because after all my foot was still broken. Sometimes as men, we let our ego and pride get in the way. But having no job and bills to pay, it was a no brainer for me to put the ego and pride aside and see if I could get my old job back. I spoke to my lieutenant, Ortiz, and told him what happened. He then told me he needed some time to figure things out. Ortiz called me the next day and told me to come in and speak with him. Once there he said he had spoken to Thaddeus.

Thaddeus permitted him to not only hire me back but gave me a promotion and had me train the sergeants who had taken over my position since I left. In this position I would have an office; I would review reports and offer guidance to the current sergeants when they needed. When Ortiz told me this, my eyes filled with tears and I could not contain my emotion as I sat there with much gratitude. He actually left his office and closed the door behind him to give me some time to compose myself. In a matter of two weeks I went from quitting my job as a sergeant special police officer, to attending a police academy and then being kicked out of the academy, making me not only unemployed, but unemployable seeing that I was injured. Then I went to not only being re-hired, but I was promoted. It just seemed to be too much in a short period of time and you couldn't make this stuff up! I was glad to be working someplace.

My new position didn't last very long because six months later I was told that Naratoone Security needed to lay people off, and I was to be the first lay-off. Fortunately for me, by that time my foot healed and I started the academy again two weeks later. In addition, as a result of being laid off, I was able to receive unemployment compensation while I attended the academy. I felt like someone was watching over me and granting me these opportunities. In December 2003 I graduated the six month academy. I even earned the "Top Gun" award for scoring the highest marks in the firearms section of the training.

After graduating, I was hired by The Tufts University Police Department. Working at Tufts University Police Department was a completely different type of law enforcement than I was used to. I went from being a housing police officer with authority and discretion to arrest anyone who committed any arrestable offense in my jurisdiction, to now being a babysitter for college students. I went on several calls where I found students with drugs and was ordered to not arrest them. Not only was this foreign to me, but it was also illegal. Going from being a housing police officer that enjoyed looking for drugs, to not being able to make drug arrests was frustrating for me. To Tufts, the university police was window dressing. They wanted us to be on the campus looking good, but they preferred that we do as little law enforcement as possible. This wasn't my style of policing, but I needed to support my family so I hung in there.

After working there for five years I was looking for a new opportunity and I was offered a position as a federal agent with the United States Government. Their offer meant I had to take a $20K pay cut to my base pay. I figured I could make up the difference in overtime pay. In addition, this job came with a pension. At Tufts University, I had a 401k.

I spoke to my old friend Russell, who was now a financial advisor, about the difference between a pension and a 401K. He explained that with a 401k, after I retired, I'd have access to the money I saved. Sometimes depending on how I invested it could be more or less, but with a pension, when I retired, I would get a check for the rest of my life regardless of how long I lived. If I died, Russell said my wife would continue to get the checks for the rest of her life.

Russell went on to explain that there were so few companies that gave out pensions, that if I had the opportunity to get a pension, I had to take it. I spoke to my wife and the next day I gave Tufts my two-week notice. As a collateral duty, I am also a firearms instructor. I not only teach the federal agents in my organization to not only shoot more accurately, but to think more tactically as to avoid a force on force situation. The United States Government considers me an expert in the use of force. Things were really getting better for me because I also got a part-time job at the Somerville Housing Police Department as a police officer. In my spare time I teach a Basic Firearms Safety Course.

15

By no means the end

This is by no means the final chapter in my life. A Better Life will become the best life ever. As you journeyed with me to this point of my life, I must extract and share with you those significant and life changing events, which I feel helped to mold the man that I am today. First and foremost was the decision of my parents Enga and Tony, specifically Enga to give birth to me despite the odds that were presented.

"Life's Getting Better" because for me it has been getting better each year. Not everyone grows up with a silver spoon in their mouth. Many people in the inner cities are faced with adversity, sometimes right at birth. Although my family was not very supportive, I did learn how to survive and navigate through the maze life had before me.

The odds of me and to some extent my siblings growing into well-rounded adults were almost nil. As my mother grappled with the scourge of drug addiction and my father attempted to build a mini gun empire, I was forced along with my brother and sisters to generally adapt to the fast paced and uncertain situations that often created chaos in our young lives. It is an extremely dangerous and scary lifestyle especially if you're black and lived in the inner cities. My father only had one job in his life and once a gun dealer is caught and they have a felony on their record, there are little chances of ever getting a 'legit' job unless they make some major life changes.

My father became infamous in and out of prison to the point where the name Crutchfield was ridiculed and appeared familiar to one of the most hardened criminals in the Charles Street Jail as I discovered when I visited that institution as a result of my two weeks detention at the Baron Center, when I paid the price for loaning the knife I used as protection to a friend at school. The psychological fear of being in a jail cell was driven into me that day by an inmate and I swore that this Crutchfield would never see the inside of a cell from that day forward.

Though the labels that society brand people associated with the drug culture and sex trade can arguably be justified, it could not deny the deep-rooted bond that my mother had for her children. There is no way to be a perfect mother but a million ways to be a good one; and Enga Crutchfield in her own way demonstrated that her children were an extension of her. For the most part I would say we were the product of a single parent family raised mainly by our mother as the head of the household.

For most of my life I hated the fact that my mother uprooted us and moved us across the country. What I did not know at the time was that the reason my mother was in such a rush to leave Compton when I was eight years old was because the gangs in my community were getting increasingly worse. They started to recruit kids as young as 10 years old into the gangs and my mother feared Aaron was there next target. I would obviously have followed suit. Her attempting to burn the house down was her way of finding a quick way to leave Compton to save us from being recruited into a gang.

No one could ever deny the love that a mother has for her children, and for years I never understood why our lives were so unstable. The reason why we went to Los Angeles when I was 13 was because she was fleeing Boston. At that time Natasha had been taken from my mother by the Department of Social Services and she thought they were going to take Aaron, Kim and I as well.

Leaving Boston and going to Los Angeles before the Department of Social Services investigation reach the point that they were going to take all of us away from my mother was her way of keeping the family together. My mother is not a woman free of mistakes, errors or regrets, none of us are. When my mother thought things around us were starting to "get hot", (her words not mine), she moved us across the country to protect us.

The reason why we left California and left John in the house was because John had started doing crack cocaine with my mother. Before this, John was the provider in the family. Because she thought his drug use would get out of hand coupled with her drug use she decided that she needed to separate from him. Because their love was so strong she also knew that he would convince her to stay if she told him her plans to leave him. Therefore we left in the dark without telling him.

When we were living on Fayston Street, what she thought would happen did happen. John convinced her to come back to him. Luckily Kim and I were able to convince her that we were responsible enough to fend for ourselves and she left us there alone. Unless you've been in a situation where you were 16/17 years old and were living on your own in secrecy, it is something that you simply can't understand. Had the Department of Social Services discovered we were living alone, we would have found ourselves in the foster care system. At the same time, the odds that my mother would have been criminally prosecuted for abandonment were equally high. It was a gamble, and luckily it paid off for us. These are just a couple examples of my mother making questionable decisions for the love of her children while fighting her addiction. We can argue whether she did the wrong thing or not, but had I not had the foresight to navigate the situation in real time, I could have easily fallen into the trap of drug sales, gun sales, human trafficking or violence.

Although they never got married, Enga and John dated for a long time. John was a heavy drinker. His drink of choice was White Label. He could drink all day and night. I could never tell if he was drunk. He drank while doing everything. He drank while fixing cars, while driving cars, while driving eighteen-wheelers, it seemed he always drank. Therefore it was not surprising that when John was in his fifties, he developed cirrhosis of the liver, and at the same time started to use crack cocaine. I assumed that he started using crack as a result of being around Enga. When I was just twenty-nine years old, John died of cirrhosis of the liver. There was a reasonable attendance at his services. There were a lot of people there that I didn't know. Even John's twin sister, Janet came up from Atlanta. Approximately twenty minutes after I got home from the services, my home phone rang and

Enga was on the other end crying. No one ever called me on my home phone looking for me, so I knew it couldn't be good. After briefly exchanging hellos, she blurted out in between whales of sorrow,

"John was your father!!!!!"

I didn't think I heard her correctly, and asked her to repeat it again and she did. I said well this is a great time to tell me, why did you choose now to tell me? She said Janet told her that she had to tell me and if she didn't tell me, Janet would call me personally. It made complete sense. We're both vertically challenged, which explained my short stature. Tony is tall 5'9". On reflection there were a number of similarities. Our work ethic was strong, and the way he took to me, even more than my siblings.

All I could say was "Okay thanks for telling me." I said goodbye and hung up the phone. I was very disappointed that she waited until his death to tell me this. I guess though I was fortunate to have now known the truth. There are so many men, and women, walking around now who have no idea who are their fathers.

I think it's important to have a supportive and loving spouse. It's also important to remember that when you get married, not only are you marrying your spouse but their family comes with the deal. My wife Gilda's family is as much my family as they are hers. Sometimes Gilda thinks her family is more my family than hers. Gilda is an incredible woman, an awesome mother and my best friend. She has always supported me. Without her support, I don't know where I would be. We have been married for 20 years. We have a child of our own, Toni who I have a very close relationship with. We both communicate very well with each other. Even when I discipline her, she knows I do it because I love her. My daughter has studied ballet, tap, jazz, and lyrical dance for twelve years. She is now studying Muy Thai, Boxing, and Jujitsu. Like her father she also enjoys shooting, which makes me very proud of her. Women and girls should know self-defense and proper weaponry usage. We go to the range and shoot a minimum of 100 rounds every week. She is truly a daddy's girl. She attends a charter school and is in the eleventh grade. She wants to be a math teacher.

Now, regarding the remainder of my family Aaron is a corrections officer for the State of Massachusetts. He was married, but unfortunately he and his wife were unable to make things between them work. He has a daughter Erin and a son Aaron Jr., from a previous relationship.

Natasha is forty-five years old now. She is still homeless and is a prostitute in Boston. She has been addicted to crack cocaine for more than 20 years. I attempted to start a relationship with her some time ago, but discontinued shortly after because I could not handle the type of stress she brought.

Kim has five sons ranging in age from 23 years old to five years old. Kim is a state certified daycare provider. She runs her daycare center from her home and is married for the second time to an awesome guy who is a Boston firefighter.

Enga stayed addicted to crack for the next 25 years. Although she has some significant medical issues, she has been cocaine free for the last 10 years. She has Chronic Obstructive Pulmonary Disease, (COPD), and can't walk more than a few paces without becoming out of breath, but she is trying to do the right thing which I am happy about. I will continue to support her as long as she stays on this path of a clean life.

Tony is still running the streets of Boston pimping women. He continues to be addicted to heroin and has the AIDS virus. As a result of his continued use of drugs, I don't associate with him, and he is not permitted to be around my family.

I am no one special in the sense of someone coming out of a very unstable background and making a great life for themselves. There are thousands of stories like mine. You just don't hear about them because they may not have been recorded in a book. It's important that true stories such as mine are shared. There's a whole new generation coming behind me who may need this encouragement.

Being in law enforcement, I can't tell you the heartbreaking stories I see of children with drug-addicted parents, parents in prison, homeless, or emotionally unstable because of their environment. I was very fortunate, because I made decisions that panned out to my benefit. I don't know how my life will end, but nowhere in these texts or those to come will it say "I gave up".

Author's Note

To the youth… I share my story because I believe it is inspiring. My message to you is that no matter what you see going on around you, no matter what your parents, family or friends are doing, you alone decide where your life goes.

You may encounter peer pressure and unfortunately some online or physical bullying. Just know that there is always someone willing to listen and offer you a supporting hand. If you are willing to put in the work, you can achieve success. You have an inner strength within you that can guide you when you are faced with hard decisions. I've seen children in broken families who believe that they are destined to follow some of the negative paths in front of them. I am living proof that this is not true. You can have a better life.

To the adults reading my story… Children need to be corrected, and they need responsible adults to show them that they can be in control of their lives. One person can make a difference… and everyone should try. If I can make a difference to these children, I'm willing to come and tell my story to them in person.

If you have a child that needs to hear my story, reach out to me. If you have a group of children that would benefit from me telling my story, I will be there. Thank you for reading about my autobiography and I hope that you enjoyed my life experiences.

You may contact me at Email:

AACRUTCHFIELDABL@GMAIL.COM or my Facebook Page A Better Life the Autobiography of Anthony A. Crutchfield lll.